The Social Brand

*Transform your brand
to win in the social era*

Published by:
The Social Publishing House

First edition, 2014
Second edition, 2015
All rights reserved.
ISBN: 0957657609
ISBN 13: 9780957657601

To my wonderful family

Praise for *The Social Brand*

"An essential insider's guide to creating brands fit for the 22nd century."

Atif Sheikh, Director, European Business Leader, ?What if!

"Most consumer brands simply spend tons of money to buy attention through advertising. That doesn't work so well in today's always-on and hyperconnected world. But simply slapping a few tools like Twitter and Facebook onto your existing branding doesn't work either. The Social Brand *shows you a new way to think of brand engagement. It's a proven blueprint chock full of examples of success."*

David Meerman Scott, bestselling author of
The New Rules of Marketing and PR
(now available in more than 25 languages
from Bulgarian to Vietnamese)

"The Social Brand is a must-read for everybody in business who wants to contribute—an inspiring manifesto that should and will change the way we look at brands."

Janti Soeripto, Deputy CEO, Save the Children

"If you work in marketing and still use words like consumer, target, *and* audience, *then you need to hurry up and buy this book. It might just save your job."*

Paul Kemp-Robertson, Co-founder, Contagious

"A blueprint for every brand looking to succeed in social media."
Menno Wagenaar, Global Partnerships, Facebook

"A thought-provoking book that challenges you to reconsider many of the basic principles of modern-day branding."

David Taylor, Founder and Managing
Partner of the brandgym and author of six books,
including *Grow the Core: How to Focus on Your
Core Business for Brand Success*

"The definitive guide to building powerful brands in today's social era—written by a true industry expert."

Nader Tavassoli, Professor of Marketing,
London Business School and non-executive
chairman of The Brand Inside

"Huib's unmatched background, including leading roles at Unilever, MTV, and Red Bull, give him a unique, industry-leading perspective on marketing in the digital age."

Patrick Kalotis, head of marketing, Pepsico

"Since 2006 I've had the pleasure of being 'the social media consultant' for many of the most powerful celebrities and brands on the planet... so I thought I knew a few things about the paradigm and mindset of the social age. Then I read The Social Brand and it blew me away. Huib introduced me to concepts that I now use every single day. I bought a copy for every member of staff in my business and we live by the principles laid out so brilliantly in this book!"

Mark Adams, director and co-founder of
The Audience UK, named one of the 50 most influential digital
innovators by the *Sunday Times*

social [sō′shəl]

adj

1. Attitudes, orientations, or behaviors that take the interests, intentions, or needs of other people into account (in contrast to antisocial behavior).
2. A characteristic of humans and other animals living in collective coexistence, whether they are aware of it or not.
3. Friendly or sociable, as with persons or dispositions.

brand [brănd]

noun

1. A name given to a product or service.

The Social Brand [thə sō′shəl brănd]

adj, noun

1. A brand that takes the interests, intentions, and needs of other people into account.
2. A brand that sets out to offer value and enrich the lives of other people through its products and marketing activations.
3. A brand that realizes that the only way to build a relationship with the people it cares about is to *give* them something truly worthwhile that they will want to seek out and share with others.

Foreword

I remember reading about the "10,000 hour rule" popularized in Malcolm Gladwell's book *Outliers*—the idea that you have to spend 10,000 hours practicing a skill if you want to become extraordinarily successful at it—and thinking that there was no endeavor that I could ever devote that many hours to. Then it struck me. There *is* one field in which I reached that benchmark long ago: marketing.

Marketing is in my blood. My father spent his entire career working in marketing for the multinational company Unilever, starting in the 1960s, when marketing was just coming into its own as a discipline. For as long as I can remember, my dad came home from work still passionate about what had happened that day, and I was always eager to listen. He took the entire family with him all over the world, so wherever his job took him—from Mexico City to Rotterdam to Johannesburg—and whatever marketing challenges he faced, I was in the know. At the age of 11, I "market-tested" new jellybean flavors among my peers in the schoolyard and gave my dad feedback on which flavor to launch. After dinner, he and I would watch TV spots for a new peanut butter ad campaign and decide which one would work best. I think we chose well; the campaign would later be voted the best advertising of the 20th century in the Netherlands. We pondered the problem of making ketchup bottles easier to use;

at home, we tested bottles that were, for the first time ever, oriented upside down. I loved every minute of it.

You won't be surprised to learn that I ended up pursuing a university degree in business and marketing and studying these subjects at the University of Utrecht in the Netherlands, Universidad Iberoamericana in Mexico City, and Harvard University in Boston. After I received my university degree, my dad was thrilled when I was hired by Unilever. I loved working for the company that I'd heard so much about and learned a lot working for international brands like Flora, Bertolli, and Lipton.

After six years at Unilever, I felt I wanted to bring more creativity to my job—to actually make ads myself and be responsible for my own (digital) platforms. So I moved into the media business at MTV. At MTV I was responsible for everything from strategy right up to the production of the commercials. In addition to positioning and marketing the TV channel and online and mobile platforms, I had my own internal advertising agency. I was actually responsible for a social media platform before Facebook was even around—a combination of chat rooms and ID pages. A brilliant experience.

After three years of working in media, I moved to Red Bull. For eight years, I was head of marketing for the Netherlands, Europe, and the United Kingdom for one of the most admired brands in the world. There aren't many brands out there that understand the craft of creating content and marketing activities that create a truly loyal fan base. I was proud to be able to play a key role in transforming Red Bull from an energy drinks company into the media business it is today—launching a magazine, vastly increasing our social presence, and creating our very own over-the-top TV offering.

I've now been working in marketing and media for more than 15 years and have proudly worked on more than five global brands, made more than 100 TV commercials, organized more than 50 events (and produced the equivalent amount of TV and web content), and created more than ten different web platforms. I can truly say that marketing and (digital) media are not only my job, they're also my favorite hobby. In 15 years of working in this business, I've seen from within how drastically the media landscape has changed.

Fifteen years ago, there were really only four media channels: TV, radio, print, and outdoor. The World Wide Web and mobile phones were still new, and companies rarely if ever used them to deliver marketing messages. Social networking and other social media sites had yet to emerge, and there certainly weren't any iPhones or other mass-market smartphones around. But now all of those things exist; they all compete for our attention and intensify the clutter of our lives—and demand that brands and companies find new ways of interacting with us.

Over the past decade, as these new media channels have emerged and people have adopted them *en masse,* I've watched many companies struggle to move their brands into this new digital and social era. During this period, I've been fortunate enough to work for blue-chip FMCG and media companies that have done a brilliant job of combining the traditional (but still relevant) rules of marketing with a fresh way of doing things in our new media environment.

My moment of inspiration

The inspiration to write this book springs from the moment I read *The Art of Loving* by Erich Fromm. I found that what he said about love also resonated with me in the way we do business. His most important point in the book is that, in love, we ask the wrong question. We ask ourselves "How can I make sure people will love me more?" instead of asking the more important question: "How can I develop my own ability to love?" Fromm says that we're all asking other people to "Please love me—please!" This statement is not only true for love—it's also very true for business. Probably the most asked question in the boardroom is "How can we make sure people buy us more?" Brands and products have always been about building a relationship with people, and we've been asking the wrong question in this relationship. We've always asked people to do more for us, instead of coming up with ways of doing more for them. I hope this book will inspire as many people as possible to start asking the right question.

Gladwell will be pleased to know that at this point I've spent roughly 1,000 hours discussing the topic with my dad, 5,000 hours studying the subject, and 30,000 hours working on it. This book is my attempt to condense these 36,000 hours into a five-hour read. I should point out that, while the book is based on my own experiences, it is *not* a book about Unilever, MTV, or Red Bull. All of the cases presented below are based on my experience and are subject to my personal interpretation; they do not necessarily reflect the opinions of the companies discussed.

Ultimately, who wrote this book is not what's important. It's what we—the businessmen and businesswomen who lead the brands that touch nearly everyone on the planet—*do* with our influence that counts. If we turn our brands *social,* the impact will be huge for our businesses and for society alike. The more people that join in—the more that we leverage the combined billions of dollars at our disposal for positive ends—the bigger the impact will be. So join the movement, share your successes, and sharpen the words (and actions!) of *The Social Brand* on the Web (http://www.thesocialbrand.co.uk) or on Twitter (@huibvanbockel).

But before you do that: enjoy the read. I hope you enjoy reading it as much as I enjoyed writing it.

Table of Contents

CHAPTER ONE

It starts with the right question

Judge a brand by its questions, not by its answers.

When sales are down or a company wants to increase its growth, the CEO will ask his management team to make sure that demand will rise. He'll probably ask, "How are you going to make sure people will start buying us more? Go on—*make* them!"

One of the first things the marketing director will do is check on the health of the brands in her portfolio. More than likely, she'll find one or two that have some critical positioning flaws and don't completely connect with the "target audience" anymore. The solution? Repositioning. Once the repositioning has been defined, tested, and approved, she'll head out to the ad agency and ask it to come up with a new campaign that will drive home that new positioning. The agency will come up with a creative, funny, emotional, or very annoying way to say what every campaign says: "Please think of me in a certain way." Or, actually, "Please like me—*please*!"

The key marketing challenge of our time—the social era—is to cut through the clutter and *engage with people*. Many companies try, but they all face one insurmountable problem: their brands are not ready. Such brands are still defined by "positioning", a theory coined in the late 1960s which proposes that a brand has to cut through the clutter of all the other marketing messages and find a convenient (and empty) slot in a person's mind that it can fit its message into. This insight is more valid than ever, but the solution no longer suffices, because being bombarded with 5,000 marketing messages a day means that people's brains no longer have any empty slots left to be filled—much less ones that are easy to access. Imagine if 5,000 new people sent you a friend request on Facebook *every day*. What would you do? What *could* you do? You wouldn't have time to accept half of them—even if you wanted to. Most likely, you'd start out being very annoyed; after a while, you'd simply decide just to ignore them all. This is exactly what's happening to the majority of today's brands.

On top of this, we're seeing a massive shift from traditional to social media. According to Nielsen's 2012 Social Media Report, the total time spent every month on social media in the US from PCs and mobile devices increased to 121 billion minutes in July 2012—a 37% rise over July 2011. This exponential growth continued throughout 2013 and 2014. By the end of 2013, one out of every seven people in the world had a Facebook page and nearly four-fifths of active Internet users were visiting social networks and blogs. At the same time, Nielsen reports that there's no longer much growth in TV. Social media has emerged from its infancy and is now a global force to be reckoned with.

In this new social media landscape, it seems like new platforms are entering the market every day. This is a major distraction, because it also leads marketers away from the right question. These new types of media make you ask questions like "Should I be on Twitter?", "What can I do on Spotify?", or the most recent one: "Should I build a branded app?" According to recent research by Deloitte, 80% of all branded apps are downloaded fewer than 1,000 times—meaning that not many brands are getting it right. Yes, we're putting more money into social media, but are we doing it the right way? It's not about shifting your budget to these new platforms, because *how* you reach the people who are important to your brand is not what's important; it's *what you do for them* that counts—no matter what medium you use.

For a brand to win in this new era, it has to start by asking the right question. Instead of asking people to do something for you, it's time for *you* to do something for *them*.

So stop asking the old question:

"How can we make sure people will do something for us— like think of us, like us, try us, or buy from us?"

And instead start asking:

"How can we make sure that we do something for the people who (will potentially) buy our product or service?"

The old question leads to taking—and thus *antisocial*— forms of marketing. I'd say that roughly 90% of all current spending on advertising goes toward things that are, at the end of the day, a form of taking. When someone's watching his favorite TV show and your ad bothers him halfway through, no matter how funny (you think) it is? Taking. When he's checking out a new website and a pop-up appears to get his attention? Taking. When he's listening to his favorite radio show in the morning and your message interrupts the flow of the show? Taking.

The new question makes your brand social at its core. If you were to describe a social person, you would use words and phrases like *generous, giving, takes time for me, listens to me*. The same goes for brands. If you want to engage in social media, you have to *be* social. Asking yourself how you can do something for your potential buyers will lead you in the right direction. In this way, social media isn't just another *media* channel to drive your message home in, but an *environment* in which you can engage in a *social* relationship. To demonstrate how this works, I'll introduce the concept of the *Brand Bank Account*.

The Brand Bank Account is both a simple theory and a powerful tool. Just like your own financial bank accounts, you make deposits into and withdrawals from it. The account has a running balance; if you don't put enough money in, you can't take anything out. The Brand Bank Account is a metaphor to keep tabs on how much you give to people who use your brand and how much you take. The more deposits you make, the more trust, understanding, and eventually connection people will feel with your brand. The more withdrawals you make, the less likely people are to be loyal to your brand, forgive it when it makes a mistake, or be willing to try a new product that it launches.

Once you start asking the right questions and have committed yourself to start giving with your brand, the next question is: "How can I make deposits?" It's important that you do something that's relevant to your potential buyer—but it's just as important to find out what's relevant for your brand to give. In other words, you need to determine what active role your brand can play. Giving in the wrong way could be a form of taking; think of your dad giving you the same advice over and over or your grandmother always giving you cookies that are past their expiration date. Just as in personal relationships, you can "give" with your brand in such a way that it doesn't feel like a deposit. It's not just about giving a discount, awarding a fancy prize, or donating to charity or another noble cause. Deposits have to build your product and your brand.

An important part of being a Social Brand is treating people with respect. One starting point is to change how you refer to the people who (will potentially) buy your products. Right now, marketers tend to refer to them as *consumers* or the *target audience*. Wikipedia has the following description of consumers: "Typically, when business people and economists talk of *consumers,* they are talking about *the person as consumer*, an aggregated commodity item with little individuality other than that expressed in the decision to buy or not to buy." The term *consumer* presumes that people are put on this earth solely to buy stuff. In other words, using the word *consumer* is by nature taking; it refers to what they will do for us economically, not what we can do for them. *Target audience* has a similar feel. To say that you're "targeting" someone doesn't really feel like you're looking to create a relationship, and the word "audience" implies that they're sitting at home waiting for you to speak to them—which, if you think about it, hasn't been the case for years. So let's refer to them like you would refer to a friend: as a *person*, as an *individual*, as *people*. From now on, let's call them that. I will never use the term *consumer* or *target audience* again in this book unless I'm referring to the old ways of marketing or quoting someone else.

This book is first and foremost about creating brands that are fit for the future and will grow your business in the 21st century and beyond. At the same time, "giving" feels so much more rewarding than "taking". *That's* inspirational. Everyone wants to make a contribution. Everyone wants to be social. And you don't have to give up work to do this; you can start giving in your own profession. At work and with your brands is where you can actually make the largest contribution. Currently, brands are the only entities that still have the budget, people, and global reach to truly make an impact. The future is in your hands; it's what you do with your brands and the billions of marketing dollars at your disposal that can truly make a difference.

Throughout the rest of this book, I hope to *give* you an interesting idea that will inspire you while also being fun to read. But most importantly, I hope to help you grow your business by moving your brand into the new social era and building a lasting relationship with the people you care about—and who you want to make sure care about you.

CHAPTER TWO

The start of a new business era

*Too many times, we simply do stuff because
that's how it has always been done.*

Business has reached an era in which asking the same question marketers have been asking for decades no longer suffices and the old marketing rules no longer apply. Although marketing is a very new discipline—Philip Kotler laid down the ground rules just 50 years ago—the process of bringing your product to market (and, thus, "marketing" it) goes back a long way. Let's take a look at the evolution of the discipline and where it stands now.

The product era

The product era was the first era of commerce—a time when products were sold at markets, usually by the same people who made them. Whether a buyer exchanged a few chickens for some salt pork or later paid in cash, the marketing—if it could be called that—was simply stating what the product and its potential benefits were. Fishmongers in ancient Greece probably had signs saying "Fresh Fish"!

Even after the Industrial Revolution, marketing and advertising were little more than signs or slogans that clearly stated the functional benefits of the product. One of Procter & Gamble's first brands, for instance, was Ivory Soap, sold as early as 1879. It had one main benefit over other soaps: the fact that it floated in water. Can you guess what the resulting product tag line was?

Ivory Soap. It floats.

Pretty darn clear and functional, right?

The marketing question of this era was: "How can I functionally *explain* the product I make to my buyers?"

The sales era

In the first half of the 20th century, competition grew and the focus of marketing turned to selling. Communications, advertising, and branding started to become more important as companies needed to sell their increasing outputs in an ever more crowded market. Marketing focused on communication that would persuade buyers that one manufacturer's goods were better than another's.

To stay within the P&G portfolio: in 1911, the company launched Crisco, the first shortening made entirely from vegetable oil. Its main competitor was butter. So, in the sales era, when it was key to point out that your brand and product were better than others, what do you think its payoff was?

Crisco: better than butter for cooking.

More refined marketing techniques also began to emerge. Part of the launch campaign was to give away cookbooks in which (naturally) all of the recipes used Crisco. Very clever—and still widely used today. In this same period, marketers started to take advantage of the wide availability of radio, using this medium in a way that would have a large impact on broadcasting for years to come: they created the soap opera. Soap operas, which were aimed at housewives, were aired on weekday mornings and afternoons. P&G, Lever Brothers, and Colgate-Palmolive—all soap manufacturers—sponsored the programs; hence the term *soap opera.* Not only did the soap opera usher in the era of branded content, it's remained one of the most popular formats on TV to this day.

The marketing question of this era was: "How can I make people buy me more by showing that my product and brand are better than the others?"

The marketing era

Since the 1960s, most markets have become saturated and intensely competitive. Marketing has become an increasingly sophisticated and standalone discipline. In the product and sales eras, companies manufactured products and then it was sales and marketing's responsibility to go out and sell them. But marketing gradually became the *starting* point of production. Marketing became less about stating a product's benefits or comparing it with other products; instead, companies started to build their brands around emotion and lifestyle.

Let's take a look at another successful product launched in the marketing era. In 1961, P&G brought Pampers, its brand of disposable diapers, to market. Pampers was an eminently practical product that met a clear need, so P&G started out promoting Pampers in classic sales-era style:

Pampers: Keeps babies drier than cloth.

As time went on and marketing became more emotionally based and lifestyle-oriented, in the 1970s P&G switched its payoff to:

Doesn't your baby deserve Pampers dryness?

It was also around this time, in 1963, that BBDO created the slogan *Come Alive! You're the Pepsi Generation!* This campaign was possibly the very first time that a product was identified not by its own attributes but by its customers' lifestyles and attitudes. In addition to adjusting its messaging, P&G marketed Pampers in new venues like print ads and television commercials. TV commercials for Pampers appeared during soap operas produced by P&G, such as *As the World Turns.* Later, the company added product placement in movies; for example, Pampers were featured in the 1987 film *Three Men and a Baby.* Like many other companies, P&G also took advantage of other methods of reaching potential buyers that became more widespread in the marketing era, like billboards and direct mail.

This was the time when ad agencies really took off; many of today's larger ad agencies, such as Chiat/Day (1962), TBWA

(1970), and Wieden & Kennedy (1982) were founded in this era. You could say that the marketing era was the period in which nearly all of the marketing tools that you still use today were developed.

The marketing question of this era was: "How can I make people buy me more by creating a positioning that boosts the brand's value by using emotion and associating it with a specific aspirational lifestyle?"

The social era

The social era started around the turn of the millennium. A quick snapshot of the rollercoaster ride we've been on since then:

In 1999, Friends Reunited, the first online social network to achieve prominence, was founded in the UK to help people reconnect with old school pals. In 2001, Wikipedia, the free online encyclopedia and the world's largest wiki, was launched; Apple started selling iPods. In 2002, Friendster, a social networking website, opened up to the public in the US, attracting three million users within three months. In 2003, MySpace (a Friendster clone) was launched; Linden Lab opened the virtual world Second Life; and LinkedIn, the social networking site for professionals, was started. In 2004, Facebook, created by and for students at Harvard University, came to life; podcasting began on the Internet; Flickr, the image hosting website, opened; and Digg was founded as a social news website where people could share stories they found on the Internet. In 2005, YouTube began storing and retrieving videos. In 2006, Twitter was launched and tweets starting flying around the Internet. In

2007, Apple unleashed the iPhone. I could go on and on, but you get the idea: a new dawn has arrived.

Within a single decade, the media landscape has fundamentally changed, and with it the way people interact with each other and with brands. But have the brands and businesses fundamentally changed *their* behavior? More platforms are appearing every day, but the problem is that *the way brands use these media* has not changed at all—they're simply transplanting old ways of marketing to these new types of media. For example:

- Product placement isn't only on TV or in films, but also in video games.
- Billboards no longer only appear on buildings or roadsides, but banner ads—the online equivalent of billboards—appear on many web pages.
- Direct mail has moved from your physical mailbox to your email inbox to your mobile.
- Not only are TV ads shown on TV, but they also roll before your online video content begins.

You can no longer employ the tried and true marketing solutions you've always used to meet the challenges you face in this new social era. Four challenges stand out:

- **The continuing rise of clutter.** By the age of 35, the average person will have seen more than 60 million ads and other marketing messages. Everyone already knows exactly what brands want from them and why, so it's no surprise that people simply ignore the vast majority of the many "Buy me!" messages they see every day.

- **Total transparency.** We live in a completely transparent world—one where most people have blogs, Twitter, YouTube, and Facebook at their disposal. You only have to make *one* product that doesn't deliver or dissatisfy *one* client who blows the whistle, and the entire world could know within 24 hours. This makes it very difficult to claim product benefits that are hard to prove or which don't really exist.

- **The dominance of social media.** Until about 15 years ago, your media mix was a combination of TV, print, outdoor, and radio. These are all so-called "lean-back" forms of media; people had no influence over the content, regardless of whether it was delivered via books, magazines, movies, TV, or radio. They simply sat back and let the messages stream in. But those forms of media have now largely been overthrown by "lean-forward" media like the Web, games, social media, and mobile. You can't talk *at* people anymore; you have to start talking *with* them.

- **The expectation that businesses and brands contribute to society.** In 2012, Nielsen surveyed 28,000 people in 56 countries about the importance of business "giving back" to society. Two-thirds of them indicated that they would prefer to buy products and services from companies that implement programs to benefit society. In 2014, more than half (55%) of the global respondents in Nielsen's corporate social responsibility (CSR) survey said that they are willing to pay extra for products and services from companies that are committed to having a positive impact on society and the environment; that's up from 50% in 2012. This trend is even more pronounced among young people. So the future is pretty clear: the majority of the global population expects companies to take a socially responsible role and is even willing to pay extra for goods and services from firms that fulfill that promise.

This new era isn't just asking for new tactics or new strategy; it's asking you to behave in a totally different way. You have to fundamentally shift your business thinking toward engaging people and beginning relationships with them.

The marketing question of the social era should be: "How can I engage the people who are important to me by doing something for them? What can I give them that they will value?"

CHAPTER THREE

The Brand Bank Account: why brands need to stop taking and start giving

Brands can't talk their way out of something they've behaved themselves into.

So you've now landed in the social era. What does this mean for the way you do business? How can you reach and engage the people that are vital to your business? In an era of superclutter, you can't just start screaming even louder; screaming louder in an already noisy marketplace will annoy rather than engage. Total transparency means that you can no longer create beautiful brand worlds around your product that aren't grounded in the truth. And the fact that people expect companies to have a positive impact leaves you asking, "How can we do this? How can we connect it with our product in a credible way?" Above all, the dominance of social media, where people choose whom they talk to and engage with, means that people have to *want* to listen—and when they do, you'll have to tell them something or give them something they love. And don't forget to listen to them too. So the answer to all of these questions is a simple one: do something that people will truly appreciate. Give them something of value. Make a deposit.

To help you along with this—not only as a tool but also as a simple reminder—I'm going to introduce the Brand Bank Account, which will indicate how much your brand gives (deposits) and how much it takes (withdraws) from the people who are important to you.

How does this work? It starts with your first and most important deposit: your product. That's what you ultimately give. This has always been the case, since long before you needed any marketing to sell it. You make a product and give that to people (deposit); in return, you charge a price (withdrawal). If the price is too high, you don't have a positive balance to draw on and your product won't sell. Your second deposit is the value of your brand. You can charge a premium price (withdrawal) if the value of your brand (deposit) enhances the product. Then the question arises; how do you build that brand value? In the marketing era this was mainly done with disrupting forms of advertising, like TV ads or radio ads (withdrawals). This would result in a balance as depicted below.

The Brand Bank Account
in the <u>marketing</u> era

Deposits	Withdrawals
Product	Price
Brand value	Marketing or advertising that disrupts what people are doing: ✓ TV ads ✓ Radio ads ✓ E-mail ✓ Etc.

In the social era, with its superclutter, total transparency, need to contribute to society, and social media dominance, it's important to also build your brand value with marketing activations that contain value, like interesting (online) content, a branded event, or an engagement program (deposits), as you can see in the balance below.

The Brand Bank Account
in the <u>social</u> era

Deposits	Withdrawals
Product	Price
Brand value	Marketing or advertising that disrupts what people are doing:
Marketing activations that give something of value:	✓ TV ads
✓ Content	✓ Radio ads
✓ Events	✓ E-mail
✓ Engagement programs	✓ Etc.
✓ Etc.	

It is important to point out that content, events, and engagement programs are only actual deposits if people are engaged in a way that is truly beneficial for them, not only for your brand.

I'll cover all three types of deposits (product, brand, and marketing activations) individually later on. But first, I want to point out why it's important to make deposits, and why the Brand Bank Account is such a powerful tool to help you do this.

Building a relationship

The starting point for the Brand Bank Account is realizing that you have to have a relationship with the people who buy your product. The growth of subscription or "sharing" services like Zipcar, Spotify, Airbnb, and Netflix shows the increasing importance of this realization. More and more, people are moving away from a culture of *ownership* and toward a culture of *relationship*, where loyalties are tied not to a brand's products but to communities that have been built up around those products. People are becoming less interested in actually acquiring stuff. The key challenge and opportunity for brands in the social era is to build a long-lasting relationship. Or, as Nike's Stefan Olander put it, "Once you've established a direct relationship with a consumer, you no longer need to advertise to them."

And as with a personal relationship, the only way to build and strengthen it is to give as well as take. Stephen R. Covey looked at human relationships in his bestselling book *The 7 Habits of Highly Effective People*. He came up with the *emotional bank account*, which is quite comparable to the Brand Bank Account. Covey describes the trust that builds up in a relationship; it's the feeling of security you have with another human being. According to Covey, courtesy, kindness, honesty, and keeping commitments are the bank deposits in human relationships. If I consistently make deposits, I build up a reserve and your trust in me grows. I can call upon that trust many times if I need to; even if I make a mistake, if my emotional bank account has a positive balance, the accumulated trust will compensate for it. Withdrawals are when a person shows you discourtesy or disrespect, like cutting you off, overreacting, ignoring you, betraying your trust, or threatening you.

In the end, every time you interact with someone else, it either adds to or subtracts from the overall amount of trust in that relationship. Covey believes that the longer a relationship lasts or the closer it is, as in a marriage, the more deposits you have to make to keep the bank balance of trust in positive territory, as you may be making automatic withdrawals in your daily interactions without even being aware of it. It's the same in business; when you have weekly or even daily contact with people via your products, advertising, or retail outlets, disappointments are bound to happen. So the more contact you have, the more deposits you have to make. The last thing Covey says about the emotional bank account is also very true for the relationships between companies and buyers: there's no such thing as a quick fix. Building and repairing relationships are long-term investments.

Trust

Just as in a human relationship, trust is the foundation of every product and brand. You can't be in a relationship with someone if you don't trust them. One human relationship in which trust is of the utmost importance is the relationship between a doctor and a patient. Unfortunately, mistakes happen in this relationship. In his book *Blink,* Malcolm Gladwell beautifully explains some of the unique and interesting research that has been done on this subject. According to Gladwell, the risk of being sued for malpractice has very little to do with the number of mistakes that a doctor makes. Analyses of medical malpractice lawsuits show that there are highly skilled doctors who get sued a lot and doctors who make lots of mistakes but never get sued.

In other words, patients don't file lawsuits because they've been harmed by shoddy medical care; patients file lawsuits because they've been harmed by shoddy medical care *and* something else happens to them. This "something else" is apparently how the doctor treated them on a personal level. Again and again in malpractice cases, patients say that they were rushed, ignored, or treated poorly—regardless of what the quality of the actual medical care was.

This is also true for brands. Brands that actually make time for people and treat them with respect and dignity are the brands that people trust and fall in love with. And if the goal of marketing is to build a relationship with people, they will have to trust your brand. In the age of transparency, this is more important than ever.

This is even true with young people. While you might be inclined to think that they want brands to be cool or opinionated, trust is the foundation of your relationship with young people as well. There's a lot of research that backs this up. For example, InSites Consulting recently asked hundreds of people between the ages of 14 and 24 what they looked for in brands. "Trust" was the top answer by far—and six of the next seven were about honesty, authenticity, and even feeling safe. The cool stuff like "glamorous" and "rebellious" only scored 3% and 6%, respectively.

Probably the biggest difference between a brand/person relationship and an interpersonal relationship is that people aren't stuck with a brand forever, like they are with their family and friends. Of course, one can end a relationship, but everyone knows that's a painful process. To decide to stop seeing a family member or end a marriage isn't something that's decided overnight; even ending a relationship with a Facebook friend is difficult. (That's why Facebook makes sure people don't see it when someone unfriends them.)

On the other hand, a brand is very easy to dump if it does nothing for the people who buy its product. If your brand has only been withdrawing from its Brand Bank Account, people will stop buying it. And that, right there, is the strongest tool people have at their disposal. When people stop buying your brand, you react by making your TV ads more urgent, screaming: "Buy me, buy me, *please* buy me! Please!! HELPPPPP!!!!" Unfortunately, your brand can't talk their way out of something it's behaved itself into. People tend to ignore such pleas and will only respond to actions. Only if your brand changes the way that it *behaves* will people change their opinions and renew their trust in it.

Making deposits to build your Brand Bank Account

It's important to point out that trust is not the goal, but rather the means to an end; eventually, you want to build a deeply rooted relationship with people who buy your brand on that foundation of trust.

Trust has become a prerequisite for the success of a brand or product, rather than a way to differentiate oneself. This is the biggest difference between the Brand Bank Account and Covey's emotional bank account. The latter has just one goal: to build up trust. But the Brand Bank Account goes beyond the basic building block of trust to encompass every aspect of your brand's business.

When people flew on a plane in the 1940s or 1950s, arriving at the destination in one piece was probably high on their list of concerns. Obviously, people still want to arrive alive, but fully expect that British Airways or American Airlines—or any major carrier—will deliver on that promise. When someone chooses whether to buy a ticket from BA or AA, they probably won't take "getting there in one piece" into consideration; they'll probably make their choice on the basis of things like price, service, legroom, and dining options.

Making deposits into the Brand Bank Account is the most powerful way to build up brand attributes on top of brand trust. *Making a deposit* is simply a metaphor for giving people something they will truly appreciate. There are many kinds of deposits you can make, each of which can reinforce a different aspect of your product or brand. Every brand should come up with its own unique way to give. Find something that's a genuine form of giving—something that's truly relevant for people to receive and which builds your brand at the same time.

A truly innovative and relevant new product from a brand is clearly a deposit. When I bought my first iPod in 2001, I loved Apple for the fact that I could now put my entire music library in my pocket and listen to it whenever and wherever I wanted. Another clear deposit is when a brand launches a new service. Ever since Google Maps came on the scene in 2005, I can't tell you how many times I've thanked Google for helping me find a great restaurant or my way back to my hotel in a new city. Every single time it's helped me out (for free!) was a deposit in Google's Brand Bank Account. And every deposit that Google makes, the more likely I am to stay loyal to the brand and the less likely I am to ever start using, say, Bing.

It could also be a great marketing activation like one I remember from Domestos, a Unilever brand that's a market leader in toilet cleaning products. At many festivals, going to the toilet is considered the absolute worst part of the event. A bad festival toilet experience has three components: you have to wait; you have to pay; and once you've finally made your way past those two barriers, it's dirty and disgusting.

So what did Domestos do? It took responsibility for the entire toilet experience at festivals. It increased the number of portable toilets, so there was no waiting time; and it made them free. Those two ways of giving alone could give people a positive impression of the brand. But Domestos also made sure that it kept those toilets very, very clean. That's also a way to give, but more importantly it was an activity closely tied to Domestos' products and was a logical step in building the brand. The first time Domestos did this, everyone at the event was talking about it and loved the brand for it. So it's clear that marketing giving isn't limited to good causes—it's about finding something truly worthwhile and memorable that only your brand can do and builds it in the direction that you want to build it. Which is exactly what Domestos did: first, it showcased the product (if it can clean a "shitload" of public toilets, it should have no problem cleaning your private one!) But Unilever also went the extra mile and built up the other components of the Domestos brand—aspects like surprising, friendly, and generous—and the relationship it has with the people going to "the Domestos toilet".

Many brands and companies are looking for ways to give, but many of them are having trouble truly connecting it to their brand and product in a credible and authentic way. An example of this is Pepsi's "Refresh Your World" campaign. On the one hand, it's great that the brand donated an astonishing $20 million in the first year of the project. On the other hand, it just feels like Pepsi is giving away a huge amount of money without in any way connecting it to their product and its benefits. Is it building the value of Pepsi's brand and product and, as a consequence, building the business? Based on the fact that Pepsi quietly pulled the initiative and given the continuing decline of its share of the US cola market, I'd say no, it isn't.

I want to emphasize that the deposits I'm talking about are not limited to good causes or traditional CSR efforts; rather, it's doing anything that people will truly appreciate that's close to your brand and builds it. Deposits come in all shapes and sizes.

So you can make deposits with your product, your brand, or your marketing activations. In the next chapter, we'll start looking a little more closely at the first deposit: your product.

Summary and critical question

Summary

In the social era, you have to engage people to cut through the clutter and build a relationship. To do that, you have to start asking yourself what *you* can do for the people that are important to you—and the best way to do that is by making deposits. There are three deposits in the marketing mix: your product, your brand, and your marketing activations. In an ideal world, there's only one withdrawal: the price you charge.

The foundation of your brand and product lies in the trust people have in it. Just as in a human relationship, your brand simply won't flourish without trust. And just as in a human relationship, the only way to build that trust is by making deposits. The more relevant and unique the deposits you make, the more connection people will feel with your brand. The more connection they feel, the more loyal they will be and the more inclined they will be to try your new product innovations—and the more successful your brand and business will be.

Critical question

Before you learn how to make deposits and avoid withdrawals, quickly, off the top of your head: What deposits has your brand made in the past year that offer true value to the people important to you?

CHAPTER FOUR

The product: the first deposit

Advertising is the price you pay for having an
unremarkable product or service.
(Jeff Bezos, Amazon.com)

In marketing and business terms, your product is what you ultimately give. This is what people go out and buy and pay a certain price for. The starting point of any Brand Bank Account is depicted below.

The Brand Bank Account
the foundation

Deposits	Withdrawals
Product	Price

But products got pushed into the background during the marketing era. Brands responded to the massive market competition and global reach of mass media in that era by creating beautiful worlds around their products and using advertising to drive that positioning home. Now, the super-clutter and transparency of the social era will force you to return to the most important aspect of your business: your product.

Let's look at a couple of the most successful companies in the world right now: Apple and Google. In 2013, Apple ranked #1 and Google #2 in Millward Brown's Brandz Global Top 100. The study, commissioned by WPP and conducted by Millward Brown Optimor, identifies and ranks the world's most valuable brands by their dollar value, a number it arrives at by analyzing "financial data, market intelligence, and consumer measures of brand equity". Apple and Google must be doing something right—so let's take a look at their approach to products.

Google focuses entirely on its products. Vice president of marketing David Lawee says that he doesn't have to do much of the usual care, feeding, and policing of the brand, let alone run any TV or print ads. "Essentially," he says, "Google subscribes to a philosophy of branding by *doing*: creating products that many people love rather than shouting about them in ads." How does Google think about its brand? "The honest answer is that the first thing we think about is our products. First and foremost, we're always thinking about what's best for the user."

The importance that Apple puts on its products can easily be distilled from many of the great quotes of the company's late founder, Steve Jobs:

"You need a very product-oriented culture. Lots of companies have great engineers and smart people, [but] there needs to be some gravitational force that pulls it all together."

"Sure, what we do has to make commercial sense, but it's never the starting point. We start with the product and the user experience."

The better your product is, the less traditional (taking) advertising you have to use to sell it. Or, as one of the most successful entrepreneurs of our time, Jeff Bezos of Amazon.com, put it: "Advertising is the price you pay for having an unremarkable product or service." Jobs and Bezos were #1 and #2, respectively, on *Harvard Business Review*'s "Best-Performing CEOs" list for creating the most long-term value for their companies. Clearly, these men know what they're talking about.

So let's have a look at what makes a good product, using Jeff's company as an example.

Three foundations of a successful product or service

The dot-com boom of the late 1990s saw the founding of a huge number of Internet-based companies. These companies saw their stock prices skyrocket if they simply added an "e" to the beginning of their name or a ".com" to the end of it. Some of them succeeded and exist to this day, but many others failed spectacularly, usually because they had no business plan, no technology, and no experience—in other words, no product whatsoever.

Flooz.com is a great example of a spectacular dot-com failure. The company's idea was to create an alternative online-only currency (Flooz) that people would use instead of their credit cards. Once someone acquired a hoard of Flooz, he could use it at any number of retailers that had agreed in advance to accept it. I often wonder if the guys that launched Flooz actually thought they had a product (but were very bad marketers) or if they were just fooling around. Either way, they thought that a celebrity endorsement might help, so they aired ads with Whoopi Goldberg saying: "Flooz. Just what you wished for." (They *must* have been kidding, right?!?)

There was just one small problem: no one had bothered to ask why anyone would use a completely new and unproven currency instead of cash, credit cards, or gift cards, all of which were backed by trusted merchants. In the midst of the dot-com frenzy, Flooz managed to raise an astounding $35 million in venture capital. Not surprisingly, the company lost all of it and plunged into bankruptcy in 2001—it came crashing down just like the majority of dot-com enterprises. The cryptocurrency Bitcoin, launched in 2009, may yet prove that a digital currency can work in the 21st century—but back in 1999, Flooz had forgotten what so many people forget when starting a business or launching a new product or brand: create a *new, relevant* product that *delivers*.

One company that got it completely right was Amazon.com. Amazon was founded in 1995, just before the height of the dot-com boom, and has since grown to become one of the world's premier online retailers. Why?

1. **It was totally new.** In 1994, Netscape released the Navigator browser, later introducing SSL encryption to enable secure transactions. Pizza Hut launched online

ordering, and some cars, bikes, and adult content were being sold on the Web—but that was the extent of Internet commerce. Amazon was the first "real" online store—and certainly the first online bookstore.

2. **It was relevant.** Naturally, new isn't enough; Flooz was definitely new, but the company never addressed the next question: is it relevant? Amazon was definitely relevant, and on many levels. First, it was closer than your local bookstore; you didn't even have to leave the house. Second, while the largest brick-and-mortar bookstores and mail-order catalogues offered somewhere in the neighborhood of 200,000 titles, Amazon—free from limitations on retail shelf space and the need to publish paper catalogues—could offer far more. Third, books were easy to find and were, for the first time ever, automatically recommended to you via the much-copied "If you like this, you'll probably also like…" mechanism— a powerful tool that's still widely used today.

3. **It delivered.** Once you've created a product or service that's new and relevant, there's just one final step to take care of: make sure you deliver on your promise. Amazon delivered—literally! *It just worked.* People could easily find books they liked; the company delivered them to customers exactly when and how it said it would. It sounds very simple and logical—but you'd probably agree that many companies just don't get this right.

These three components of a product or service have always been very important factors in your product's success in the marketplace. But now, to succeed in the transparent and cluttered social era, you have to add two more: *transparency* and the ability to make your product's message *easy to grasp and to communicate*—or as I will refer to it later; the ability to "tell it in a tweet".

Transparency

The most obvious prerequisite to becoming a Social Brand is being transparent about what you're doing, making, and selling. What do you think the biggest withdrawals in a human relationship are? Most people would put lying, cheating, and covering up the truth high up on their list. Well, the exact same thing is true for brands. There's no greater withdrawal than not being transparent. And today, in the social era, where the power is with the people, transparency isn't just good practice—it's an absolute necessity. With 180 million people using social media in the US alone, you only have to make a small mistake—like trying to hide something or make something look better than it actually is—and someone will blow the whistle.

Let's have a look at two recent marketing activations in the same industry. One is good; the other's just plain ugly.

Domino's Pizza

No brand has taken transparency as far as Domino's has—although this move was born of necessity. In April 2009, the chain was taken by surprise by a YouTube video showing employees doing disgusting things in a Domino's kitchen. The incident forced Domino's CEO Patrick Doyle to post an apology on YouTube. You might think that this would have caused the company to shy away from social media. But it did the opposite, hiring the agency Crispin Porter + Bogusky to create a new campaign called "Pizza Turnaround" that showed actual focus groups describing the pizza crust as "cardboard" and the sauce as "ketchup". In the ad, Doyle vowed to do better and to overhaul Domino's products. The campaign was a hit; sales increased by double digits in the first quarter in which the ad ran.

In 2011, the pizza chain put up an electronic ticker in New York's Times Square with a real-time display of what people really thought of the brand. The huge digital billboard showed *all* customer comments—good, bad, or neutral (they were only filtered for language and appropriateness). The comments were taken directly from Domino's Tracker, a way for people to track their pizza orders online. If your comment was chosen, you received a link to a video clip of the comment as it ran on the ticker. The chain ran a concurrent TV campaign showing two New York-based Domino's store managers reacting to seeing the comments in Times Square. This "take it as it comes" approach may have been brave or may have been foolhardy, but Domino's felt it was necessary to revamping its image.

The digital billboard gave Domino's the chance to reinvigorate the Tracker, which allows the more than 40% of people who submit their orders online to track their food from the oven to the front door. Once the order has been delivered, people can rate their experience and leave comments. "We'd had this tracker for about three years, but we felt it was time for a coming-out party," said Domino's CMO Russell Weiner. Although the Tracker received mixed reviews, Domino's kept it, believing that it was fundamental to the chain's image makeover. "We're a pizza company, and our pizza needed to be better," said Weiner. "That's a tough thing to address."

And Domino's kept going with the "Show Us Your Pizza" campaign, promising to skip the fancy food photography and use unretouched pictures of its pizzas in its advertising—another effort to be transparent that makes a deposit. And it doubled down on this promise by asking people to upload photos of actual pizzas they received to ShowUsYourPizza.com for a chance to win cash and have their images used in an ad campaign. It wasn't long before people had uploaded more than 30,000 images of Domino's pizzas.

Weiner feels that the biggest lesson from Domino's turn-around would apply at most big companies. Brands already know what their biggest weaknesses are; they don't need someone from the outside to point it out to them. He added: "I hope that what people have taken away from this is not just that transparency works, it's that figuring out what your core issue is, and taking it on is the way to do it."

#McFail

Another fast food chain also had a go at transparency. McDonald's tried to jump on the social media bandwagon by launching a campaign featuring paid tweets that would appear at the top of search results. This was part of a larger effort to tell the "transparent" background stories of the fast-food chain's personnel and suppliers. Unlike Domino's, which actually listened to and shared everyone's comments, McDonald's thought it could create its own edited stories on Twitter. It created the hashtag *#MeetTheFarmers* to accompany wholesome stories about farmers to promote the company's guarantee of fresh produce. For example, McDonald's tweeted:

> *Meet Dirk Giannini, McDonald's lettuce supplier, as he shows u his life on the farm #MeetTheFarmers*

Everything was fine until the global chain sent out tweets with the more general hashtag *#McDStories*. The tweet read:

> *"When u make something w/pride, people can taste it," - McD potato supplier #McDStories*

But within minutes, the tweets started going way off-message and the hashtag took on a life of its own. Detractors pounced on *#McDStories* as a chance to share their supposed Golden Arches horror stories, such as:

> *Watching a classmate projectile vomit his food all over the restaurant during a 6th grade trip. #McDStories*

One of the worst tweets was:

> *I haven't been to McDonalds in years, because I'd rather eat my own diarrhea.*

These two examples show how important it is to be genuinely transparent. And transparency isn't just about a marketing campaign or the quality of your products—it's also about the overall environmental and social impact your company has. There are already some good tools to measure your transparency and company policy on these issues, such as MSCI's environmental, social, and governance (ESG) Intangible Value Assessment research. According to MSCI, "Institutional investors are becoming increasingly aware of the potential risk and value impact of these factors and their potential effect on an investment profile. ESG factors—from environmental practices to labor standards to regulatory compliance—can have a material impact on the long-term risk and return profile of investment portfolios."

Tell it in a tweet

In a time of superclutter and online sharing, the ability to make your product's message *easy to grasp and to communicate* is of great importance. If you want your product to "tip"—if you want people to promote it—your message has to be really easy to convey. The more words you need to explain your product's unique benefits, the more advertising you will need to sell it. As a consequence, you'll always need to "take" a lot to get your message across—depleting your marketing budget and Brand Bank Account in the process. A great way to test if you can explain your product in a concise and compelling way is to see if you can "tell it in a tweet"—that is, using 140 characters or less. If you can tell it in a tweet, you know it will be easier to grasp and easier to share. To help you understand how to do this, let's have a look at an industry that boasts some of the masters of short-form messaging: Hollywood.

Learning from the movie industry

"Once he was the general of the Roman army; now he leads the slaves in the lion pit." Immediately, you feel the tension in that statement; it sounds like something you want to see. And if you've seen the film, you immediately know that the sentence refers to the Oscar-winning box-office hit *Gladiator*. We can learn a lot from the way Hollywood works. It uses something called "high concept" to pitch projects. High-concept refers to the technique of being able to sell an entire movie in one sentence; it takes what we in the business world call an "elevator pitch" to the next level.

In the movie industry, not only should the idea for a movie be easy to convey, but you should also immediately feel that "I want to go there!" the moment someone tells you about it. If you can tell an entire story—whether it's about a movie, product, or brand—in a compelling way in 140 characters, you've got a winner. The people in Hollywood knew this decades before Twitter came along.

Big investments on the basis of a single sentence

In Hollywood, developing the product (the movie itself) is a very expensive proposition; producers and investors have to decide if they want to sink $200 million into a film on the basis of an idea. Of course, there's a difference between a nobody coming to them with a great idea and Steven Spielberg doing the same. But even Spielberg won't get them to invest $200 million if he doesn't have a great idea—and that idea has to be crystal-clear and compelling within the space of a single sentence.

The benefits of a message that's short, sweet, and to the point are obvious. But why would anyone make an enormous investment decision on the basis of a single sentence? Two reasons.

The first reason: with a movie, studios can't see or test the product until they've already spent most of the money. Investors can realize a return of up to $1 billion if the film is very successful, but there's no way to be sure. Even Virgin's Richard Branson thought that the movie industry was too risky to invest in—and that says a lot. Branson flies hot-air balloons across the world and has made large investments in many new and unknown markets—yet he bailed out of the film industry after bankrolling a couple of movies.

The second reason that studios determine whether to make a big investment on the basis of one sentence: that's how moviegoers will judge if they want to see the film. Studios realized long ago that word of mouth is a key element of the success of a movie. People reading that one sentence in a movie or TV guide or on the back of the DVD box will have to be convinced by it. We can try on new clothes before we take them home, listen to a new song we like on YouTube or Spotify before deciding to buy it, and take a potential new car out for a spin, but when it comes to movies, we have to settle for a couple of sentences or a trailer. So if you can't convince a movie producer in one sentence to back your film, there's no way you can convince millions of people to go and see it.

Let's take a look at a couple of sentences describing some well-known recent movies:

- An aristocrat whose life was devastated when he was paralyzed in an accident hires a black Muslim ex-con as his caretaker. Their unlikely bond proves that friendship can transcend socioeconomic differences.

- Two very good friends (a man and woman) add casual sex to their relationship. But they soon discover what the rest of us already know—it gets complicated.

Each pair of sentences captures the entire movie perfectly (for non-cinephiles, the first is *The Intouchables* and the second one is *Friends with Benefits*). If it's possible to sell a two-hour movie in a couple of sentences, it should be possible to sell a new product or service in one sentence. If you want to make your product successful, it has to spread; if you want it to spread, it has to be easy to share; and if you want it to be easy to share, you have to be able to tell it in a tweet.

This way, you can set aside your company's long innovation pipeline techniques and PowerPoint presentations and let all of your employees tell or tweet you their new idea in one simple sentence, because that's exactly how everyone else will hear about it. For example, here's how to quickly describe some well-known products, both timeless and recently successful:

A beautifully designed device that fits in your pocket and contains your entire music library.

A simple, free online tool that allows you to stay in touch with your friends 24 hours a day.

A free app that makes all of your pictures look really beautiful and shareable with your friends.

An airline that flies you from London to Barcelona for €20.

Summary and critical question

Summary

The product is the first thing you'll give, so make sure you give something good. The three traditional prerequisites when launching a successful giving product are:

1. Is it really something new and unique (does it differentiate)?
2. Is it relevant?
3. Does it deliver what we say it does?

The social era has added two new prerequisites:

4. Is the product completely transparent?
5. Is the product's message easy to grasp and to communicate? Can you tell it in a tweet?

Critical question

Check how you score on all five prerequisites for a successful giving product. In particular, look closely and honestly at the two new prerequisites:

- Is the product 100% transparent? Make a list of all the things you think you should be transparent about. Examine the product's entire supply chain.
- Is the product's message easy to communicate? Sell your product convincingly in 140 characters.

CHAPTER FIVE

Building the brand: from a "positioned brand" to a Social Brand

Stop positioning—find your mission and start giving.

Your first deposit is your product, to which you can add brand value, which in turn allows you to charge a price premium, as shown below.

The Brand Bank Account
adding value with a
Social Brand

Deposits	Withdrawals
Product	Price
Brand value	

The question is: How can you do this in the social era? How can you build a valuable, differentiating Social Brand? It's important to be social, but it's just as important to find out what it is that you—and *only* you—can give.

Defining your brand mission

Every company has its own way of capturing the brand essence or positioning of the brands it owns. For instance, Procter & Gamble uses "brand equity", PepsiCo uses the "brand pyramid", and Unilever uses the "brand key". Each of these methods is based on the old marketing-era term "positioning".

Positioning

To repeat what I said at the beginning of the book: positioning is basically the process by which marketers try to create an image or identity in the minds of their "target market"; advertising is the tool they use to create this image.

The way companies position brands today goes back more than 40 years. The business challenges they face today are in no way comparable to those in the 1960s and 1970s— but, oddly enough, the rationale behind the need for positioning today is exactly the same as it was then. Jack Trout first wrote about this new form of marketing strategy in 1969, making the case that the typical person is overwhelmed with unwanted advertising and has a natural tendency to discard all information that doesn't immediately settle into a convenient (and empty) slot in their mind. Today's superclutter has made it outright impossible to find a convenient, empty slot in anyone's mind.

Positioning documents like the ones mentioned above focused on questions like "What kind of a brand world do we want to create in the minds of our customers?" (How does the company want to position its product or brand and communicate that positioning?) That's not good enough anymore. Instead, ask: "What kind of a world do we want to create with our brand *in the lives of people who are important to us?*" In other words, companies need to create a *social* brand by defining a mission and then actually taking on and fulfilling that mission.

Defining your Social Brand mission

There are three key elements to a brand mission: insight, personality, and mission.

The Social Brand
1. Insight: the need you set out to fulfill with your product and brand.
2. Personality: the way you go out and fulfill your mission, with what personality traits.
3. Mission: the mission you take on as a brand. What do you want to make happen in this world?

Brand insight

The principle of defining an insight does not change. It's a key element of every positioning statement and remains just as important when defining your mission. This insight should naturally be based on the people you have in mind that will buy your brand. It should also be the clear insight, or need, that your product fulfills. In other words, you need to explore and understand the human needs, beliefs, and behaviors behind your product and brand. Why do people need it, use it, or like it?

The principle hasn't changed—but how you *define* it should. Keep your mission in mind when defining your insight. Think about what need you want your brand to go out and fulfill. Don't shy away from defining a "higher" or "bigger" insight.

If you want to define a "higher" insight, you can use Maslow's hierarchy of needs as a starting point. Define your insight around the three lower needs: "basic needs" like food, water, sleep, and sex; "safety needs" like security, order, and stability; and "love and belonging needs". The latter are psychological needs; when people are taken care of physically, they're ready to share themselves with others, such as family and friends. The majority of today's brand insights are still defined around the three needs at the bottom of the pyramid.

You can also to choose to define your insight around the top levels of Maslow's pyramid. "Esteem" is the fourth level, achieved when people feel comfortable with what they have accomplished; it's the need to be competent and recognized, as through status and level of success. "Need for self-actualization" sits atop the pyramid; it's what occurs when people reach a state of harmony and understanding because they are engaged in achieving their full potential.

So how would this work for a brand?

- A sports brand could define its insight around "basic" and "safety" needs, pointing out the need to exercise or look good. It could also define itself around the need for self-actualization—for someone to reach her maximum potential through sports.

- A computer brand could position itself around "safety" or "love and belonging" needs—being able to keep organized or connect with others. It could also define itself around being able to creatively leave one's mark in the world.

- A bank could set itself up as a guarantor of safety, positioning itself around security, order, and stability. It could also base its insight around customers' drive to be successful or accomplish their life goals.

Brand personality

The brand personality is the way you go out and fulfill your mission. A Social Brand is, by its very nature, a personal brand. So if you were to define the brand as a person, what personality traits would he or she have?

The key element to take into account is not mistaking the personality for the positioning (or, in the new world, the brand mission). Stating that the brand personality is very strong and reliable doesn't mean that you have to create advertising *saying* that your brand is strong and reliable—it means that you should go out and fulfill your mission in a strong and reliable way.

Clearly defining the personality of your brand mission is important because more and more brands are or will be defining an active social mission. There will always be brands that have the same mission, so you have to define a clear personality to ensure that you are unique and differentiating.

The three most important aspects to take into account when defining your brand personality are *authenticity, purpose,* and *consistency.*

Authenticity

"Authentic" is probably the most used—and misused—word in marketing today. How many brands have the word "authentic" in their brand personality? I'd guess there are only a handful that don't. Being authentic is knowing who you are and staying true to that. Therefore, your brand personality should be defined as who you are. Not just that *you* are authentic—that's an obvious thing to do.

The first step in being authentic is matching your personality to your brand. Ask yourself: "What do I stand for? What is it that I would like to leave behind in the world? What really matters to me?" I think that this is a great exercise to do before you start working on your brand—because if there isn't anything of you in the brand, it's not worth working on. Of course you should not change the brand to fit to your personality, but find something genuinely interesting in the brand personality or mission that resonates with you.

Next, it's important to clearly and concisely define what the personality of your brand is. It's important to define this, because many different people work on a brand, both now and in the future. Again, compare the brand with a person. We always want to know what kind of people our friends are; it would be very strange if they suddenly started wearing different clothes or liking totally different music. It would feel like they weren't being real, like they were selling out. Authenticity in brands is also very important; this is why some of the strongest brands in the world were defined by one person: their founder. This makes the brand genuine and consistent.

Some great examples of brands defined by their founders are Apple (Steve Jobs), Nike (Phil Knight), Virgin (Richard Branson), and Spotify (Daniel Ek). These brands are based on their founder's personality—that's why they always feel "right" and authentic. For example, Richard Branson is clearly a man who likes to spice things up. And that's usually where he does the best job—in areas that could use a little spice, like the aviation industry, where he made life tough for powerful established players like British Airways.

Phil Knight is another example. Julie Strasser, coauthor of *Swoosh*, wrote that "Nike for Phil Knight is not something he does. It's something he is." According to the book, in high school, the young Knight was too small to play contact sports, so joined the track team. When his father refused to give him a summer job at his newspaper, Knight went to the paper's rival, *The Oregonian*, where he worked the night shift on the sports desk and ran the full seven miles home every morning. Not long after that, he founded one of the most successful and iconic brands in history. Knight is clearly a man who "just does it".

This doesn't mean that no one else could ever take over and do a good job, but it will be difficult. This is not only because these people are brilliant at what they are doing, but also because you have to find someone else who *is* the brand.

According to Jobs, "Apple's core value is that we believe that people with passion can change the world for the better." He was not only talking about Apple, but also about himself. He said this back in 1997, and I think he's been proved right. He revolutionized personal computers, animated movies, music, mobile phones, tablet computing, and digital publishing. Now that he's passed away, the question is whether his successor, Tim Cook, has that same drive and passion to change the world. If not, the brand will either change its personality or start feeling less authentic.

So: be authentic. Know who you are, know what your brand is about, and stay true to both of these.

Purpose

To define a personality that's not only close to you personally but also stays close to the product, look at the purpose of your product. Your brand and product should have an essence to them—a purpose for which they are made. The man who masters "the art of purpose" like no other is John Lasseter, the chief creative officer of Pixar and Disney and the man behind blockbusters like *Toy Story* and *Cars*. All of the characters in his movies have an essence to them, whether they are toys or cars. As for toys, Lasseter's original treatment of *Toy Story* began: "Everyone's had the traumatic childhood experience of losing a toy. Our story takes the toy's point of view as he loses and tries to regain the single thing most important to him: to be played with by children. This is the reason for the existence of all toys. It is the emotional foundation of their existence."

We can easily translate this idea to (branded) products—just look at the products from their point of view. Imagine what a product would feel if it had feelings and was driven by a desire to fulfill its essence. The purpose of a washing powder, for example, is to clean clothes; if it had feelings, it would be happy when all the clothes were clean and smelled fresh, and it would be sad if the clothes came out of the washing machine dirty and smelly. Cars are made to drive you around; your car would feel useless if you just left it parked in front of your house all the time.

There are two reasons why it helps to think of the purpose of your product when defining your brand personality. First, as with insight, purpose is key to keeping the brand and product close together. Imagining the purpose of your product is a great starting point for coming up with the right personality statements—statements that will make your product come alive and ensure that the brand and product are automatically linked in people's minds. To stick with the *Toy Story* example: if Woody were a brand (and, given that about 25 million Woodys have been sold and theme parks have been based on his character, we can comfortably say that he is) and we were to formulate his personality traits based on his purpose as a product (a toy cowboy), we might choose traits like *wise, faithful,* and *charming.* For a product like Quaker Oats, we could say that the purpose of oatmeal is to fill you up, comfort you, and keep you going until lunch. Projecting those onto personal characteristics gives us traits like *warm, comforting,* and *strong.*

The second reason that it's important to add purpose to your personality is that it humanizes your brand. You can only build a relationship with a brand if it has a human aspect to it, because only then will you recognize something of yourself in it, be inspired by it, and possibly even fall in love with it.

Consistency

If you're authentic as a brand, it automatically means that you're also consistent, because you always stay true to who you are. All strong brands are consistent; they stay true to who they are while at the same time adapting themselves to new times, new media, and their own product innovations. Consistency has always been important, but—as with so many other marketing activities in the social era—it has become more difficult. Being consistent on TV, on the radio, and in print is a lot easier than being consistent across the wide range of media channels available today. But that's exactly the reason why it has become even more important; in a time of superclutter, consistency makes you easier to recognize and thus easier to maintain and build awareness. But being consistent doesn't just support your brand awareness; it also enhances your familiarity and likability.

Robert Zajonc proved this with his "mere exposure effect" theory, a psychological phenomenon where people tend to develop a preference for things merely because they are familiar with them. Zajonc tested the mere exposure effect by showing meaningless Chinese characters to two groups of people. These people were then told that the symbols represented adjectives and were asked to rate whether they had positive or negative connotations. The test subjects consistently rated symbols that they had previously seen more positively than those they had not seen. After the experiment, the group that had been repeatedly exposed to certain characters reported feeling better and more positive than those who had not. Since then, the effect has been demonstrated using things like words, paintings, sounds—even people.

Another interesting fact that Zajonc pointed out is that, once people have decided that they "like" something, it's very difficult to sway that opinion. Everyone believes that they're experts on themselves and that they know what they like—regardless of whether they've consciously backed up that feeling with evidence.

However, it's hard to stay consistent for the simple reason that every new CEO, CMO, or marketing team will want to leave their mark. Often, this means that the newcomers try to change something that they think isn't working as well as it should or test their own pet theory.

A classic example of consistency is Marlboro. The "Marlboro consistency" story is a famous one; anyone who has ever worked there could probably tell it to you. Whenever a new marketer came along, he would perform extensive market research and would always come to the same conclusion: "the cowboy" doesn't work anymore. The man with the hat alone on a faraway mountain was old-fashioned and no longer appealed to young people; he'd simply lost his edge. The marketer would take his story to headquarters and present it to management, along with tons of research to back it up, and confidently announce that only one conclusion could be drawn: the cowboy is the problem! Senior management always had a very simple answer: "No, son, the cowboy is the answer." Based on experience and the outstanding results that the brand had enjoyed, management knew that the consistency of the Marlboro brand would trump any new idea, no matter how potentially powerful or fun it was. Other brands that have found success in consistency are Nike and Apple; both companies still work with the same agency they started with more than 30 years ago (Wieden & Kennedy and Chiat-Day, respectively).

Brand mission

Once you've defined an insight to base your product and brand on and found a personality that stays close to your product and yourself, it's time to define your brand mission. Here is where you can really transform your brand into a Social Brand. It's no longer about finding and communicating the right positioning; it's about finding your mission in life and asking yourself how you can actually go out and make that mission happen.

Defining a mission that matters

To repeat: this book is first and foremost about creating brands fit for the future to grow your business in the 21st century and beyond. But people now expect companies and brands to have a positive social impact—and that will be even more true as time goes on. As I mentioned earlier, this is a key element of the social era. In the Nielsen survey I referred to in Chapter 2, 55% of people surveyed across the globe said that they're willing to pay extra for products and services sold by companies that are committed to having a positive impact on society and the environment. If we decide to make our brands social, defining an active mission and committing to making it happen, there will be a wider (and necessary) impact. It's vital to base the definition of your brand mission on true insights and align it with your product—but don't shy away from defining a mission that matters.

More and more people are getting behind the notion that brands can and should make a positive difference. In his book *Religion for Atheists*, philosopher Alain de Botton argues that "the supernatural claims of religion are of course entirely false— and yet religions still have some very important things to teach the secular world." He argues that the church imbues us with higher motives, like inspiring us to be kind, to value community, and to have a sense of perspective. As the church has declined as an institution, many people have tried filling that void by writing philosophical or inspirational books or holding workshops and gatherings. But to change attitudes and behaviors and contribute to complex and significant issues, you need institutions.

De Botton points out that, in this day and age, we still have institutions with the power that the church once had: large corporations. Only companies and brands have the budget, people, and global reach to make that kind of an impact. But he points out that they have so far failed to take on that mission. He believes that companies and brands must take responsibility, define an active "higher" mission, and put all of their efforts behind that mission to make it happen. In other words, he explains why brands need to become *social.*

Someone who has also embraced that philosophy is Nicola Kemp of *Marketing* magazine. In an article about Red Bull Stratos, the project in which Felix Baumgartner broke the sound barrier, she wrote:

> *The success of the Red Bull Stratos project underlines a broad cultural shift in marketing, where brands are attempting to improve society, not just their bottom lines. People have described Felix Baumgartner's jump as an astonishing display of the value of human endurance, of adventure, investment, and commitment.*

> *8 million concurrent views on YouTube prove amongst others that this was a feat nobody wanted to miss. The fact is, Red Bull both created and funded a mission to the edge of space that will create data and insight that could benefit NASA. As one viewer tweeted: "That awkward moment when you realize an energy drink has a better space program than your nation."*

Consumers may have expressed discomfort at David Cameron's vision of Big Society, but Red Bull Stratos raises difficult questions about marketing taking off where government funding ends. "Red Bull has taken science forward and no one is questioning it. Whether you agree that this will benefit NASA or not, there is no doubt that it is fueling a passion for science," says Sav Evangelou, executive creative director at Kitcatt Nohr Digitas. He believes there is a huge opportunity for brands to carry this shift forward if they can share knowledge or deliver progress to society, whether it is through education or investment.

Philosophers like de Botton and journalists like Kemp both challenge marketers to take their companies and brands forward and dare to make a difference with them. Stop positioning; define an active mission that matters; and put all of your company's passion and effort behind it to make that mission happen.

Defining a Social Brand mission

Your mission is about defining what you want to create for others with your brand—that is, what you want to make happen. In the case of positioning, you would ask, "How can we tell people about our new positioning?" But once you've defined your brand mission, the key question you need to ask is "How can we take this mission out into the world? How can we make it happen?" Two examples of companies with crystal-clear brand missions are Nike and Magazine Luiza.

Nike

Nike has moved from inspiring (mainly via its TV ads) to enabling. The company is committed to its brand mission and has set out to make it happen. Nike's brand mission is "to bring inspiration and innovation to every athlete in the world", and it makes sure to point out that "If you have a body, you are an athlete." Nike has made this mission clear in words: "Just do it" and, more recently, "Make it count"—but more importantly, the brand's actions show that it's committed to this mission and pay-off. For example:

- **Awareness.** Nike's "designed to move" platform is an action agenda for physical activity. It argues that the first ten years of a person's life provide the foundation for a lifelong commitment to physical fitness. Nike teamed up with the American College of Sports Medicine and the International Council of Sport Science and Physical Education to design this agenda. The Nike Foundation also released a film called *Extra Time,* which asks kids what they would do with the "extra" years of their life that they would gain by being physically fit, interspersed with shots of abandoned playgrounds and broken goalposts.
- **Events.** Nike sponsors events like the Nike London Run, which inspires and enables many Londoners to run.
- **Digital platforms.** Nike creates digital platforms like Nike+, which says it is "the best way to track, share, and compare your runs and connect to the world's largest running community. Get the push you need to keep going farther and faster." Nike doesn't just say it, it does it.

Magazine Luiza

Magazine Luiza is a family-owned electronics and home furnishings chain in Brazil. The Brazilian middle class now numbers 118 million people, and retailers are clamoring to reach out to this new demographic. In order to support these people, it's important to enable them to find affordable, high-quality products close to their new homes. One of the most successful at it is Magazine Luiza. The company's brand mission could be defined as "giving as many Brazilians as possible the opportunity to own the quality furniture and electronics that they need to simplify and improve their quality of life."

Magazine Luiza's mission, and the company's commitment to that mission, is clear from its actions—in this case, its innovative and social approach to stores:

- **Experience retail.** Magazine Luiza realized that shopping is a social activity in Brazil, so the company invested in so-called "concept stores"—hosting events from cooking courses to technology product demonstrations.

- **Virtual stores.** Ever since the 1990s, the company has faced the problem of expanding throughout a huge country without expending a massive amount of money on brick-and-mortar stores. So it created a virtual store—a physical store without any inventory. Sales associates use computers to guide customers through the company's merchandise; the goods themselves are then shipped directly to customers' homes.

Virtual stores allowed the brand to build a monopoly in rural areas in a way that made economic sense. One hundred stores later, it's still a viable solution to help people who lack a credit card or high-speed Internet to "shop online".

- **Magazine Você.** Again faced with the dilemma of how to increase sales without building new stores, the company took a genuinely social approach to online retail (*magazine você* is Portuguese for "your store"). Its platform allows members of Facebook and Orkut (the national social network) to create their own mini-stores online and stock those stores with up to 60 items from Magazine Luiza's inventory. Magazine Você "owners" can then sell these items to their friends and collect a commission of 2.5% to 4.5%; Magazine Luiza handles payment processing and delivery. To date, more than 53,000 stores have been set up and have sold more than 10,000 products between them.

Testing your payoff

A great way to test if your brand is a Social Brand is to take a good look at your payoff. Are you just saying it—or are you actually committed to it? There are two ways to check this. First, where does most of your brand budget go—toward withdrawals or deposits? (We'll discuss this in more detail in Chapter 7.) Second, what's your intention? Usually, this shines through quite clearly no matter what type of media type or to what degree a medium is "social". Let's have a look at two well-known payoffs:

Coca-Cola: "Open Happiness"

Coca-Cola makes some great deposits. It has a clear sponsorship strategy, including its longstanding sponsorship of the Olympic Games. The brand also has many strong corporate projects, such as its goal to support five million women entrepreneurs worldwide by the year 2020.

However, I believe that Coca-Cola will still spend most of its budget on withdrawals, the vast majority going to traditional advertising. The advertising in which people "open happiness" makes it clear that it's just something the brand says—something it assumes will happen naturally when you open a bottle of Coke. The company doesn't make it clear that it's undertaking actual projects to help people "open their happiness".

As I write this, Coke's last five Facebook posts have all been about its new polar bear ads. The brand's first post of 2013 was:

> *Happy New Year! The Coca-Cola #PolarBears are back! Watch them first here…*

Attached to the post was Coke's new polar bear ad. After three days, the post had exactly 289 likes—a rather underwhelming response from its 57 million "friends". Using your Facebook page to show your new ad is apparently not what "friends" consider something of value. It just goes to show that it's not about the medium you use, but how you use it.

Verdict: it's simply a (positioning) statement.

Nike: "Make it count"

As I've already mentioned, Nike has a clear brand mission and is committed to making it happen. It's a nice example to use again in this context, because if we look at Nike's Facebook page and check what it shared over the New Year, you can see a real difference in commitment and a clear connection with the level of engagement the brand gets. Nike's New Year's post was:

We give our best to get the best from you. That's how we take you further. Get your friends. How will you #makeitcount together in 2013?

Attached to the post was an inspirational picture of running people and a longer motivational quote. Nike has "only" 11 million followers, yet 4,713 people liked this post in the first three days. The company combines the necessary inspiration with the tools mentioned earlier to help people make something good happen.

Verdict: it's a commitment.

Summary and critical question

Summary

Define your brand mission. Keep it very simple so that your whole company (and everybody else) gets exactly the same message. This also makes it easier to execute the mission. Make sure it matches part of your own personality, so that it feels close and "authentic" to you. Your brand mission has just three building blocks:

1. **Insight.** Explore and understand the human beliefs and behaviors behind your product and brand. Why do people use it, need it, or like it? Don't shy away from defining an insight higher up on Maslow's pyramid.

2. **Personality.** What personality traits does your brand have? It's very important to point out the difference between personality and mission once again: the mission is *what* you go out and do (the most important part of your brand), whereas the personality is *how* you do it (reliable, fresh, glamorous, etc.). The three key traits to take into account are *authenticity, purpose,* and *consistency.*

3. **Mission.** How can you fulfill your insight? What is it that you want to claim and go out and support people with? Make sure that your mission is unique and differentiating.

Critical question

Do you have a brand mission in place, or have you defined your brand in terms of positioning? If you don't have a brand mission yet, define one. Make sure to give it insight and personality. Again, make sure that your mission is an active one—one that you commit yourself to and really fulfill.

CHAPTER SIX

Maximizing the link between brand mission and product

Anyone can create 20% extra brand value—for free.

One of the key difficulties in creating a Social Brand is keeping your brand mission close to your product. The urge to create a beautiful social mission can be strong, but if it doesn't link back to your product, it won't build your brand or business. This was easy back in the day when you could still simply say *Ivory Soap. It floats.* Now, with the need to take on a mission that matters, it's clearly become more difficult—but if you get it right and maximize the link between your brand and your product, amazing things can happen. See below how this could build your Brand Bank Account.

The Brand Bank Account
maximizing brand value

Deposits	Withdrawals
Product	Price
Brand value created via your brand mission	
20% extra value by maximizing the link between brand and product	

I remember reading a story in *Reader's Digest* when I was very young that has stuck with me ever since. It went a little something like this:

Back in 1920 in a small town in Indiana, there was an old man with a very big machine. This machine was specially designed to remove any kind of wart. A single five-minute treatment and your wart would fall off three days later—guaranteed. The man and his machine had never been wrong. People from all over the country would visit him, sometimes bringing their family members, all wanting to get rid of those unsightly bumps. Wearing his white lab coat, the man would take you into his office and show you the machine, which filled half the room and had something that looked like a stick on the end of it. He would describe how special it was—that it was the only machine in the world uniquely designed to do just one thing: to remove warts.

The man then put you in the chair, told you to sit tight, and reminded you that the wart would vanish in exactly three days, making sure to repeat the day on which this would occur. Then he would turn on the machine, which produced a loud, terrible noise, took the stick attached to the machine, and pressed the hard, cold end gently against the wart for exactly five minutes—not one second less or more.

He would then send you off with a smile and a pat on the shoulder, congratulating you on the disappearance of your ailment. And what do you know: three days later, you would wake up and check your hand—the wart was gone!

In the last days of the man's life, his son wanted to take over the thriving family business and asked, "Dad, how does your machine work? And how do I fix it if it breaks?" The old man replied: "Well, son, it broke 50 years ago, and it's made that terrible noise ever since. And the machine's never worked better!"

This story is a great example of mind over matter. If you induce a strong, compelling belief and expectation in someone, an effect can occur without any real medical intervention. At the time, *Reader's Digest* said that this account of the man and his machine was based on a true story. And the scientific facts back this up: seven out of ten warts disappear without any medical intervention. But the man's patients didn't know this; they thought the machine had cured their warts. In medical terms, this is called the *placebo effect*. But you could also call it a very strong brand. Because the old man with the big machine did everything a good Social Brand should do: he took his patients seriously, treated them with dignity and delivered on his promise. He was rewarded with a great reputation and a high degree of trust in his ability to get results.

Psychology has always intrigued me, and "mind over matter" stories always score high on my stickiness list. So I asked myself: Could this work in the field of marketing? Is it possible to create an effect or sensation that isn't actually there? Or, to put it another way, is there a way to enhance the effect, taste, or sensation of your branded product? I believe that there is—and there's research to back it up.

The extra 20%

When I started my career, my marketing director called all of the marketing people from all of the company's brands together. Representatives of more than 20 "A" brands were present; all told, there were more than 200 people in the room. An enormous number of products was laid out for us. Right then and there, we were all challenged to take blind taste tests of our own products. Not only did the director want to see if we could recognize our own products (products that we were working 50 or 60 hours a week to market), but also which products we thought tasted or worked the best. In every category, we tested our product, another A or B brand, and two private labels of large supermarket chains. All 200 people had to try everything, so the group as a whole yielded nearly enough data points to constitute real quantitative research. The results were devastating: our brand only won in a single category. This is exactly what our marketing director wanted to prove at the time—and after the session, we got the clear message that this was not acceptable. We had to get back to work fast and make sure that every one of our products was the best choice in a blind test.

At the time, I was impressed with the marketing director's initiative to get all of us out there in view of the entire company and challenge us with our own products. I agreed that the results were bad and that we had work to do. But we were also doing something *right*. Even as we were judging our own products to be inferior to those of our competitors, many of us had market research on our desks proving that our brands easily won taste tests when they were not blind. When people could actually see which brand they were eating or drinking, we nearly always came out on top.

When you do your marketing right, your product should come out stronger in the non-blind test than in the blind test. And this is exactly what happens with the good brands. When I first heard of this phenomenon, I was astonished. First, I thought it meant that people just *thought* that it tasted better. But no—people actually judge the taste of products based on many different taste characteristics. And when they see that it's an A brand, they actually judge that it tastes better. This "extra taste appreciation" is absent in the blind tests.

The difference between the blind and non-blind tests is what I'm referring to when I talk about "the extra 20%". If your product scores better in a non-blind test than in a blind test, your brand has successfully created this extra 20%. This means that your brand has created an experience, taste, or feeling that enhances your product—something that is not perceived without the brand.

To find out more about this phenomenon, I spoke with Pieter Punter, founder of the research agency OP&P, to get insight into how to create this extra 20% and what the theory and facts underlying the idea are. Since founding OP&P more than 20 years ago, Punter has worked with companies like Heinz, Mars, and Unilever and overseen more than a quarter of a million taste tests. Of these 250,000 tests, about 40% were branded and 60% were not branded. This makes Punter one of the most experienced men in his field; he knows the effect that product quality and brand strength have on the perception of a product like no other. He knows how to create this extra 20% for a brand. His 20 years in the field have shown him just how difficult product differentiation is, as the differences between brands—even between A brands and their private-label, B-brand, and C-brand competitors—have gotten smaller and smaller. It's harder now for brands to beat the competition—so you need your brand to help you out. But (and Punter and I agree on this point) it all starts with the product. Punter couldn't think of any examples from the past 20 years where a company was able to use a good brand to compensate for a bad product. What he *has* seen is that good brands can make very good products even better—and bad brands can make good products worse.

Before we go into this, it's important to understand OP&P's methods. Test subjects answer questions about intrinsic product attributes like bitterness and sweetness, but the core question is about *likeability*. People have to judge a product on a seven-point scale that runs the gamut from "very bad taste" to "extraordinarily good taste". In the course of 250,000 tests, Punter has found that strong brands can increase the number of people checking one of the top three boxes by 15% to 20%. Think about that for a minute: you can move 20% of people from neutral to good or from good to very good or extraordinary. Imagine the competitive advantage you'd have and its subsequent impact on your sales!

The first question is how this effect is possible. How does it work? Punter says: "The best comparison that can be made is with wine. If you do a blind taste test with wine, many people can't even distinguish between red, rosé, and white wines. But if you test wines 'non-blind' and see that you're going to drink a red wine, your brain opens up a 'red wine book' that tells you what tastes to look out for. You could say that your brain is actively looking for red wine characteristics; if they are there, it will distinguish between those tastes." It's been said (by Seth Godin, among others) that a brand can create a placebo effect. Punter disagrees: "If your brand emphasizes, say, creaminess, that's what people will be looking for. If it isn't there, a countereffect will occur; people will be disappointed. On the other hand, if people do perceive the creaminess, they will rate the product a lot better because they're actively looking for it in 'that creamy brand.'"

So the first very important learning point for products and services is that you can't create a taste or a feeling that is not actually there. Therefore, your first goal should be to have a product that is at least as good as those of your (cheaper) competitors. To repeat: *you cannot make a bad product good.* This sounds logical, but Punter also sees that A brands are increasingly concerned with the entire brand world, while the cheaper brands (which only have their products to lean on) are overtaking A brands in product performance.

The last question I had for Punter: Can this extra 20% only be created for taste enhancement, or could it also apply to other categories? He was convinced that all kinds of brands can attain it. Functional products like Becel margarine, which claims to lower one's cholesterol, can do it. In Becel's case, you can directly compare the margarine's cholesterol-lowering effects with a medical placebo; if people are convinced it will lower their cholesterol, the chances are higher that it will.

This effect can also occur in categories where experience is a large part of the product—like the car industry. Automakers know that they can enhance certain effects by, for example, creating an extra sporty engine sound. Even if you're never going to drive that new sports car at 200 kilometers per hour, you'll be a lot more satisfied if the engine sound gives you the *feeling* that you're driving 200 even when you're only going 100. Nearly all automakers have sound engineers working on every different sound aspect of the car. The robust, solid sound that a Volvo door makes when you close it creates an impression of reliability; the high-pitched sound an Alfa Romeo engine makes signals high performance. This has all been designed and crafted by a sound engineer to give you a better experience.

Creating the extra 20% with giving marketing

One of the most difficult questions in marketing is how close you have to stay to your product when marketing it. According to Punter, you have to stay *very* close—always. At the same time, I want to emphasize that staying close to your product with your brand does not mean that your advertising has to remain purely functional and only focus on the product. You can, for example, use an inspiring mission that you want to go out and fulfill in this world to build up that very important product attribute.

Ben & Jerry's vs. Haagen-Dazs

Let's look at two fierce competitors: Ben & Jerry's and Haagen-Dazs. These two brands are very comparable; they both produce exquisite, great-tasting ice cream that they sell in the same size containers at roughly the same price. I heard some interesting facts about these two companies that fed directly into my theory of the power of Social Brands. I tested this theory on a group of 300 people (again, enough to qualify as quantitative market research).

The first question I asked the group was: "Which ice cream do you think has the stronger brand?" All 300 people went for Ben & Jerry's—an amazing result! This wasn't a scientific study, so I told them that they were right, at least based on the number of friends Ben & Jerry's had on Facebook—about a million at the time. Haagen-Dazs, on the other hand, had only been able to gather about 700 friends, most of which were probably employees. Then I asked which brand had made more deposits into its Brand Bank Account. Which of the two would have a higher positive balance? Clearly, it's Ben & Jerry's, a company with a long history of making deposits with its brand. All 300 people knew this. My third question was whether they would rather work for Ben & Jerry's or Haagen-Dazs. Everyone replied "Ben & Jerry's"—proving my point that working on a brand that gives is much more fun than for a brand that does not.

Now came the really interesting question: "Which company makes the better ice cream?" Nearly everyone chose Haagen-Dazs!

There are two interesting conclusions that can be drawn. First of all, it shows that you can build a very strong brand with giving marketing by making deposits. The two brands have a roughly equal global market share (if we take distribution out of the equation). Before I conducted this "market research", I had learned that Haagen-Dazs beats Ben & Jerry's in (branded, non-blind) taste tests of vanilla ice cream (the most important flavor); this was confirmed by the 300 people I asked. So we know that most people think Haagen-Dazs tastes better. Even so, based on their market shares, we can conclude that half of the people choose Ben & Jerry's simply because of the connection that they feel with the brand.

The second conclusion is that Ben & Jerry's could do so much better. Apparently, Ben & Jerry's wins all of the *blind* taste tests against Haagen-Dazs. This means that Ben & Jerry's actually tastes better! I think Ben & Jerry's could outperform Haagen-Dazs by making sure that it gives in ways that emphasizes its (better-tasting) product. Always.

Ben & Jerry's gives in many ways that builds its product and brand; for instance, treating cows (the source of the product) with great respect and fighting hard for the environment (resulting in a better planet and a better foundation for great natural ice cream). However, the brand has also chosen to give in many ways that does not build the product. For example, Ben & Jerry's currently supports the Occupy movement. The company states on its website that it "wish[es] to express our deepest admiration to all of you who have initiated the non-violent Occupy Wall Street Movement and to those around the country who have joined in solidarity." Ben & Jerry's also supports charities like WarChild all over the world. It's great to see that Ben & Jerry's sticks its neck out to support these movements and charities. But does it emphasize the most important benefit of the product? No, it doesn't.

This is exactly the reason that Ben & Jerry's loses the non-blind taste test to its single-minded (product-focused) competitor. Ben & Jerry's should make sure that all of its deposits build the main benefit: its great-tasting ice cream. Now, will the company listen to me? I doubt it; it's part of the brand's DNA to give in all different kinds of ways. But I truly believe that there are endless ways for Ben & Jerry's to give that will *all* build its product, and consequently its market share.

Dulux

A great example of a Social Brand that has maximized the link between brand mission and product is Dulux. The paint brand's mission is "to add colour to people's lives", and the payoff is "Let's Colour". The brand's actions show that it's committed to this mission and payoff. The Dulux website says that "The Let's Colour Project is about transforming grey spaces all over the world, from Brazil to France, to India and beyond—it's as much about transforming and touching the lives of people as it is about sharing the joy of bright and beautiful colours using Dulux paint." All over the world, the company has brought Dulux paint to old schools, churches, shantytowns, houses—anything that craved a bit of color. This is a great example of how you can have a giving mission while letting your product do what it does best: paint! Not only does it make a difference, it enhances the key benefit of the product: the ability to make things look better and more upbeat. It also points out the social aspect of painting: it's nice to work together to make something look better. For every project, Dulux discloses how many liters of paint it donated, how many people were painting, and how many lives were touched.

I think Dulux could do even better. It makes a mistake that many brands make: doing its giving via a separate "CSR" platform. The company launched this project on a different web platform (Letscolourproject.com) instead of integrating it into the main brand website at Dulux.com. The Let's Colour philosophy should be at the brand's core and should shine through everything it does; it shouldn't be a separate way to give. Whether you want to paint your bedroom or your local school, you should go through the same process: choose an area, wall, or room you want to paint, find the inspiration, find a group of friends, and then *let's color*.

For example, Dulux uses many famous local artists in the Let's Colour program. Why not let those same artists be an inspiration for your home as well? Also, Letscolourproject. com is about painting together—but this doesn't even appear as a topic on Dulux.com. Painting your new house with friends and family can be a bonding experience; why not create a tool on the website to invite friends to help you paint, say, your new nursery? You could upload a picture of how it looks now, invite your friends to take part, let them help you decide on the colors, and add what they'll get in return, like a nice dinner or an old-fashioned sleepover (last chance before the baby comes!).

So when you decide on your mission and what you want to give, keep it close to your product and don't just make it a CSR program. Create a mission that is consistent in everything you do, whether it affects an old church or your bedroom wall.

Summary and critical question

Summary

When creating a Social Brand, resist the temptation to stray too far from your product. If you're creative, you can think of great ways to give that build your product and brand together. If you do this well, you can improve the "likeability" of your product by 20% and boost your business in the process.

Critical question

Take a close look at all of your marketing activations. Does every single one clearly build your most important product benefit?

CHAPTER SEVEN

Marketing activations: make sure you give more than you take

Roughly 90% of all current spending on marketing goes towards things that are forms of taking.

After you've clearly defined your brand mission (and have made sure to keep it close to your product), it's time to make that mission happen. Again, the difference between the marketing era and the social era is that in the former, you defined your positioning and then communicated that positioning, primarily through advertising. To be successful in the social era, you define a brand mission and actually go out and make it happen. A mission is accomplished by its actions, or, as I refer to them, *marketing activations*. See below how this would balance out the Brand Bank Account.

The complete Brand Bank Account
in the social era

Deposits	Withdrawals
Product	Price
Brand value created via your brand mission	Marketing or advertising that disrupts what people are doing:
20% extra value by maximizing link between brand and product	✓ TV ads ✓ Radio ads ✓ E-mail ✓ Etc
Marketing activations that give something of value: ✓ Content ✓ Events ✓ Engagement programs ✓ Etc.	

Treat your marketing activation like a product innovation

When you launch your first product, or when you're adding one to your portfolio, it has to meet certain standards in order to succeed; it has to offer value to the people it is intended for. These elements are covered in Chapter 4. But now, to become a Social Brand, it's time to realize that this isn't only the case for products anymore; it's also the case for *all of your marketing activations*. A Social Brand wants to build a relationship with its (potential) buyers by making deposits in line with the brand's mission. These deposits, like product innovation, have to meet the exact same standards; they have to truly offer value.

This is a major change from traditional marketing. When you make a TV or radio ad, the ad itself doesn't have to contain value; its duty is to *show* that the brand and product it is trying to sell has value. You don't have to buy the ad, seek it out, or choose to view it; the simple fact that the ad is forced upon you while watching a TV or radio program means that you have no choice but to see or hear it.

The Marketing Era

1. Product.
2. Brand positioning: emotive/lifestyle associations "positioned" around the product.
3. Advertising: driving home that positioning with communication.

On the other hand, a giving marketing activation—whether it's a piece of content, a branded event, or an online game—has to have the same qualities as a good product, or people won't view it, visit it, or play it. The new paradigm is to treat your marketing activation as you would the launch of a product or service.

The Social Era

1. Product.
2. Brand mission: a clear definition of what you will give or deposit in line with your product.

3. Marketing activation: actions of value—deposits—that fulfill your brand mission.

You could add a fourth layer to this: the media plan. This was less complex in the marketing era. After choosing your advertising idea, you would then decide on the media to use. Nearly always, this was TV, perhaps with the addition of print, radio, or outdoor. In the social era, defining your media mix has become a lot more complex, for a couple of reasons. First, there are many more media channels and products to choose from; second, media channels—like, say, the Apple App Store—are also now choices for marketing activations. Building a plan has become much less linear and much more organic. The creation of a marketing activation now goes hand in hand with your media mix.

To sum up: there are many media channels, media products, and marketing activations that you can choose from. Many of them are withdrawals; some I consider neutral; and many are potential deposits. We'll start with the withdrawals.

Withdrawals

- TV ads
- Radio ads
- Direct email or text marketing
- Online advertising like pop-ups, pop-unders, (moving) banners, and pre-rolls (just a few of a seemingly infinite set)

All of these are, in principle, withdrawals from the standpoint that people aren't waiting for ads to happen; ads are forced upon them. They're doing something else—watching TV, listening to the radio, surfing the Web, or reading their email. The only way to continue doing what they were doing is to first sit through some ads asking them to buy this or that product.

TV ads

TV ads are withdrawals based on the fact that they interrupt people who are watching something they actually *want* to watch. No one sought the ads out or actively wanted to watch them. As I said earlier, I'm talking about ads on TV, not online ads that people actively seek out, watch, and share online. No matter how good your ad is, when it interrupts a TV show that someone was enjoying just so they can see the ad for the fourth time (as you know, 4+ will be the minimum reach target advised by your media agency), it's clearly a withdrawal.

One possible exception to this rule is "sports break advertising", such as the TV ads that air during the Super Bowl or World Cup soccer matches. You're not *really* breaking into a program just to show ads; there's a break between quarters or halves anyway, so people have to do something else to fill up that time: go to the bathroom, get a beer, analyze the match, or watch something on another channel. So it's basically their choice what to do with those minutes. If a great ad spot comes along that really entertains them, they'll sincerely say "Thank you!"

You can also make an argument that truly brilliant ads—spots that are actually better than the program people are watching—would be a deposit. Then again, once they've watched it four or more times, it will revert to being a withdrawal. A great way to see if your ad is brilliant is to see how viral it gets on its own. But then your ad is no longer "just" a TV ad, but a good piece of content that people actively want to watch. We can tell that something is really changing with ads if we look at the numbers that brands are now hitting with their viral ads.

Looking at the Top 100 viral campaigns as assessed by *Ad Age*, we can see a clear development. First of all, the sheer numbers: the top three viral campaigns in 2012 were Kony 2012, Red Bull's Stratos, and Angry Birds Space. They all went well over 100 million views during the course of the year—the first time any branded video had done so. Compare that with the year before: the top viral ad of 2011, Volkswagen's The Force, would have only come in at #5 on this year's chart with its "modest" 63 million views. The #2 viral ad from 2011, T-Mobile's Royal Wedding, wouldn't have even made it onto the chart.

Second, nearly all of the ads on the 2011 list aired on TV with bought advertising spending; the viral video was an add-on. But in 2012, more brands made video content a central part of their strategy; the top three spent no money on TV. The same names and brands continued to do well in 2013, and the video views have kept climbing: every one of the year's top ten viral videos had more than 50 million views. Although 2013 did not have a viral giant like Kony 2012 or Red Bull Stratos, Dove's Real Beauty Sketches—the viral winner of 2013—had more than 130 million views. Half of the 2012 top ten wouldn't even have made the cut in 2013! Keep in mind that brands are also paying to promote these videos, so views are a reflection of both viewer interest and the budget the advertiser is putting behind them. But the better the ad, the more it will be shared.

Third, while 2011's top three viral campaigns were all pro-duced by "traditional" ad agencies—Deutch (VW), Saatchi &

Saatchi (T-Mobile), and TBWA (Google)—2012's top three were all created in house. Alongside the trend of companies creating their own content, more and more agencies are challenging the status quo by excelling at media and content strategy and creation. Agencies like Red Bee and Caperock.tv have backgrounds in media, giving them a more editorial perspective than traditional ad agencies.

There is huge potential for brands entering this space: the Top 100 list is dominated by a handful of brands that apparently understand that not only is it free, it's also *giving* instead of *taking*. These brands are engaging in an actual relationship with the people choosing to watch their branded content. It's always the likes of Samsung (which took 40 of the 100 places!), Apple, Red Bull, Nike, and Google that rule these charts.

So: making a powerful piece of content and sharing it online? Deposit. Making an ad to put on TV, as most of the world's brands are still doing? Withdrawal.

Radio ads

These are also clearly a withdrawal. Someone's listening to their favorite song, DJ, or news program, and before they know it, they're hit by five minutes of advertising. Unlike TV ads, which can occasionally have the power to give, rarely have I heard any radio ads that were really memorable or enjoyable. But then again, you can use radio as a medium to build awareness. Remember, it is a Brand Bank Account; it doesn't *all* have to giving. You just have to make sure that you make more deposits than withdrawals.

Online ads and direct mail

Again: clearly withdrawals. Regardless of whether an online ad is a pre-roll, a pop-up, or a pop-under, no one's waiting for them to happen, no one's actively seeking them out, and the ads distract people from what they're doing. A debate is currently raging on more than 100,000 websites about which form of online advertising is the most annoying. Nearly half of the respondents to an Adobe research survey on online advertising agreed that "online advertising is creepy and stalks you" and more than half agreed that "most marketing is a bunch of BS." The average click-through rate on banner ads is on the order of 0.01%—meaning that 99.99% of people completely disregard all of the banner ads on the sites they visit. The one thing these ads actually motivate people to do? Install ad-blocking software.

Of course, one way to make your ads as relevant as possible is to make sure that they reach the right people. If somebody is doing research for a vacation and sees an ad for a hotel in the process, this is a little less taking. It's a smaller withdrawal, but it's still far from a deposit. One example I love that in my opinion is certainly neutral—and perhaps even a deposit—is WeTransfer. While you wait to send or receive a big file it serves you a beautifully designed ad, made just for WeTransfer, and the company is very strict about which ads it allows on its platform. The ads always end up being a pleasure to look at; given that they're not interrupting anything and actually entertain you while you wait, this is one of the only deposits that I can find in the digital advertising space. It is very possible—*if* you do it creatively.

Neutral media

This category comprises media forms that are neither withdrawals nor deposits. These are what I call "neutral" media. Saying that a promotion is neutral means that a person can be exposed to it without interrupting or distracting him from something he was already doing like a TV ad or online pop-up does—but at the same time, it's not giving him any real value. The three media channels that I consider neutral are:

- Billboards
- Cinema ads
- Print ads

Billboards

Billboards are a neutral medium. Say someone's waiting for a train; while she's waiting, she can check out the billboards in the station. Sure, one could say that billboards are a form of pollution; some people are annoyed by constantly seeing advertising in our cities and along our highways. But the point is that billboards don't interrupt anything that anyone's already doing; thus, they start from a neutral standpoint. Now, turning this neutral standpoint into a deposit is something else entirely. But sometimes it's simply nice to know that there's a new product on the shelves or to get some inspiration for what to have for dinner. Or you can use a billboard to actually inspire people. As Alain de Botton argues, being surrounded by inspiring, positive messages will help you be positive and inspired. In other words, it's easier to turn a neutral form of marketing into a deposit.

Print ads

The exact same thing can be said for print advertising: no one *has* to look at them; they can simply choose to stick to the articles. I sometimes get annoyed by the fact that the actual magazine content only starts on page 20 or so, but the fact is that we're all used to it and expect nothing different. Also, magazines in particular can offer advertisers a specific group of like-minded people, meaning that the ads can more readily be tailored directly to readers' interests. Above all, print ads don't actively interrupt the reader while they're in the middle of a great article—so we can consider them neutral.

Cinema ads

Movie trailers shown before the feature film starts are also fundamentally neutral forms of promotion; they actually build the excitement a little and make people aware of other movies they might want to see. Just like billboards and print ads, there's no interruption—just a delay before the movie begins—so cinema ads can also be considered neutral.

Deposits

Now for the deposits. Many forms of promotion *could* be deposits but frequently aren't. So I'm going to give you an extensive list of media channels and products that have the potential to give; for each media platform, I'll add an example that I believe is giving. Many of these examples come from the news and intelligence feed provided by my favorite marketing innovation consultancy, Contagious.

- Services
- Giveaways
- (Concept) stores
- Brand events
- Engagement programs
- Digital engagement programs
- Sponsorship
- Apps and games
- Social media
- Your own digital or social platform
- Internal resources and expertise
- Content

Services

A beautiful example of a great (and important) deposit is what India-based lighting brand Halonix did: it turned its billboards into streetlights in an attempt to make India's streets safer. Crime against women is on the rise in many Indian cities; according to government statistics, crimes like rape, dowry deaths, abduction, and molestation rose by more than 25% in New Delhi in 2013—a problem exacerbated by poorly lit streets. Halonix saw an opportunity to help women feel more at ease on the streets and worked with Cheil Worldwide (India) to make it happen. The result was the Safer City Project, which launched in the second half of 2014. They started with a post on Halonix's Facebook page asking the people of New Delhi to identify the city's darkest, most dangerous streets. The brand took the collected suggestions and created an online poll asking people to vote for the streets that were least safe and were most in need of extra light.

Once the most dangerous streets had been identified, Halonix set up billboards and kiosks fitted with high-lumen Halonix products that turned into streetlights at night. This is a great example because the brand clearly found "a mission that matters", kept it super close to its product, gave it a memorable tagline—*The Right Light*—and used a great marketing activation to get the word out. And when you do things right, people notice: the media picked up the story and the positive response impelled the brand to roll out the idea in seven other Indian cities. People have since called for the campaign to be expanded even further across the country.

Giveaways

Giving something away is, in principle, a deposit. Giveaways come in all shapes and sizes, and not many of them are very memorable. You can either give your own product away as a form of sampling or give something away *with* your product. It never hurts to give something away for free—especially now, in this tough economic climate. Sampling remains a strong tool to engage with people who will not easily risk money on a new product. As with all deposits, make sure it is has value and is relevant for you to give—in other words, it has to build your brand and product.

In November 2014, the Australian branch of credit card company American Express purchased the majority of ad space in New South Wales' leading newspaper, the *Daily Telegraph*, to give as a gift to the region's small businesses. The brand also purchased a "platinum wrap" of the paper, announcing the campaign with a letter from Rachel Stocks, the managing director of American Express in Australia. The takeover ran for one day, as part of the financial giant's sponsorship of Shop Small, an initiative to support small local businesses that accept American Express cards. In principle, this is a great deposit; it also ticks all of the boxes of staying close to the product and giving something of real value to the people who are important to American Express. The only downside from my perspective is that it feels too much like a "one-off"—more of a temporary stunt than a true commitment to small businesses. I visited American Express' website but couldn't find any mention of an ongoing commitment. In principle, this is a great activation that could easily run for many years, constantly reinforcing the brand's commitment to small businesses, boosting their bottom lines and relationship with American Express at the same time.

Another great example of giving something away that's clearly a deposit is Jana's new Mobile Rewards Platform. Founded in 2009 by Nathan Eagle and Ben Olding, Jana's platform revolves around the insight that mobile phone minutes cost more, relative to income, in emerging markets. As a result, precious airtime is becoming a currency—and phones are becoming devices not just for communication, but also for compensation. Suppose a woman in Bangalore tries a new soap. For doing so, she gets 50 rupees' (about $1) worth of airtime transferred to her handset. In 2012, Jana helped double Danone's sales by providing airtime minutes to its customers. This has the potential to not only boost advertising efficiency, but also to increase spending power; this woman will save on her mobile phone bill. Of course, the fact that she receives an actual push SMS on her mobile is a withdrawal, but the fact that she clearly gets something of great value in return is what makes it a deposit.

(Concept) stores

A brand store is giving by nature, because people enter voluntarily to either buy a product or engage in the brand world. A pioneer in this space is 22-year-old British entrepreneur Ross Bailey, who founded Appear Here, an online marketplace for shop space, in 2012. The idea itself is very giving; it not only intends to solve a problem for brands wanting to engage with people important to them, but also helps tenants who are stuck with long-term rental agreements but are not currently using the space. One of the many brands that Appear Here has collaborated with is Marc Jacobs. To celebrate the launch of its new Daisy Dream fragrance, the brand launched a pop-up shop with a difference. For three days, a "tweet shop" appeared in Covent Garden, exchanging Marc Jacobs goodies in return for tweets.

Brand events

At Red Bull, we always start with the question "Is there any person or group of people who could use an extra pair of wings?" When we've identified that person or persons, we then talk with them and start brainstorming what kind of support would be useful to them.

For example, in many countries, BMX racing was becoming more and more popular, but there weren't a lot of facilities where people could practice the sport. So we started talking with folks in the BMX scene to find out more. We quickly became aware that there was a huge shortage of good dirt trails and courses where they could ride their bikes, do tricks, and race. So we came up with the idea of the Red Bull Back Yard Digger. The concept was as follows: we sent messages via youth media and BMX Internet sites and blogs, telling BMXers that if they could arrange a place and a permit, Red Bull would help them design, shape, and build a course using our machinery and expertise. The opening was always marked with a BMX Jam.

The cool thing about it was that the two sides cooperated closely with other. It's not like Red Bull ran an ad saying "You can win a dirt-biking course; just tell us where you want it and we'll do the rest." The BMXers had to do a lot of it themselves: find a spot, get a permit from the local government, and help us dig and build. On the one hand, without their commitment, we had nothing. On the other hand, without Red Bull's support, they would never have been able to build such a spot. We brought together the world's best BMXers to not only help design the course, but also to jam together with the local riders once it was done.

Put yourself in the mind of one of those young BMXers: you love to ride, but have no place to do it. Then you hear that Red Bull will build a track for you if you arrange a spot. So you go out of your way to make it happen. Then the Red Bull team comes along—bringing your all-time BMX hero with them—and builds the track using the best machinery. When the course is done—something you're already satisfied with—then you get the opportunity to ride with your hero on your own track! I personally went to the building of two courses, and the amount of energy and pride that I saw in the eyes of the BMXers was always a very fulfilling experience.

Engagement programs

Back in 2000, companies still weren't using the Internet as a marketing tool all that often, and no real social network sites yet existed (Friendster and MySpace only appeared in 2002 and 2003, respectively). So those of us at Unilever who were working on Bertolli had to build something ourselves. Because we had an "Italian" brand, it had to be about dining with friends and family. In collaboration with a cool new agency, Lemz, we came up with the following idea.

We built a site that you could use to organize dinners. On the web page, you could invite all of your friends and assign them each a certain role for the dinner. Everyone had to prepare something. Then—and this was the most important part—we printed out the letter and sent it to each invitee's house together with an actual (tiny) bottle of olive oil. So you received a letter at home from a friend inviting you to dinner at his house, but stipulating that you had to contribute by making part of the meal. The recipe—and the olive oil to help make it—were enclosed in the envelope. On the one hand, we made it very easy for people to use a Bertolli product for the first time; we gave you the recipe and the olive oil. On the other hand, you received it from someone you liked and who trusted you to do your part to make this dinner with friends a success. We later tested how many people took part and actually prepared the requested dish: it was close to 100%.

Within three months—and without spending a cent on marketing—100,000 dinners were organized. It was completely viral (remember, this was 2000; it was still quite unique). And people mailed us hundreds of heartwarming stories—from marriage proposals made with the whole family present to reuniting friends and family that hadn't spoken to each other in years. I think this is a great example of giving marketing: instead of airing an ad that showed friends and family eating together, we made it happen. And we got results, showing that it can indeed be very effective.

Another example is a great program we ran on MTV: the "MTV Talent Pool". We let young people send in their music; each month an expert panel would choose the one with the most potential and produce a video clip (at no cost to the performer) that we would then air. Having a compelling video clip is now almost a prerequisite to breaking into the music industry; nearly all new music starts on Vevo, YouTube, and the few music TV stations that are still around. But it's a risky proposition, because there's no guarantee that your video will make it to air (only about 5% of the videos we received at MTV actually aired). So having your own video with guaranteed airtime is like winning the lottery for young musicians. The video clips were produced by talented young directors; in this way, we would not only support young musicians, but young filmmakers as well.

It's a simple concept, but people loved it. We tested the concept among a large group of people who actually made music and an even smaller group that would actually get a video clip. But we found that *everyone* loved the idea—for two reasons. First, they felt MTV's genuine commitment to talent. It wasn't a TV ad screaming "Send in your music and *one* person can win a video clip!!!" It was a long-term program—we chose a new video once a month—and the tone we used in our advertising made the artists feel that we were really committed to nurturing their talent (and we were—everyone at MTV loved the program!). Second, it was something that they could relate to. Everyone knew someone who could sing or had a band and wanted to break through, and everyone places a high value on giving people that they know personally a chance.

That's what real engagement is about: you ask people to give you something—host a dinner with friends or create their very own video clip—in a way that they will thoroughly enjoy. When someone puts a lot of effort into making an Italian dinner exactly as they want it to be, the brand becomes part of them— it becomes their own. You know what they say: no other child is as beautiful in your eyes as your own. As with your child, strong loyalty to your brand is bound to follow.

Digital engagement programs

Just like "normal" engagement programs, digital engagement programs are giving because it's an active choice to get involved and be part of a brand. Not too long ago we believed that there was not much engagement happening online. The old content paradigm was simple consumption, as encapsulated in the "1% rule":

1% of people create content.

9% of people contribute to the content that the creators produce.

90% of people passively view the content without participating.

But participation has now become the norm. Recent BBC research showed that the model that has for years guided many people's thinking in this area, the 1% rule or 90-9-1 principle, is outmoded. The proportion of people participating online is significantly higher than 10%.

Participation is now the rule rather than the exception: 77% of the UK online population is now active in some way. This has been driven by the rise of "easy participation"—activities that may have once required great effort but which are now relatively easy, expected, and everyday. The majority of the UK online population now participates in this way, doing everything from sharing photos to starting discussions.

Despite the fact that participation has become relatively "easy", almost a quarter of people remain passive—they don't participate at all. This passivity is not rooted in digital illiteracy, as traditional wisdom may have suggested; 11% of the people who are passive online today are early adopters. They have the access and the ability to participate, but choose not to.

Digital and online media have endless potential for engagement and also open up new ways to give. One thing that can really boost engagement is exclusivity. Because nearly everything on the Web is free and timeless, people now value scarcity, exclusivity, and rarity. Engineering exclusivity in digital is hard—like music that can only be played once, websites that only people with lots of Facebook friends can access, or exclusive content that only a lucky few know about—but it can be rewarding. Brands that can engineer experiences that emulate scarcity, rarity, and reward social connectedness will come out as winners.

Brands can also find novel ways of using people's social networks to spread the word. A great example of this was the release of Swedish rapper Adam Tensta's song *Pass It On*. There's only one "copy" of the song, and it's only available via a Facebook app. Once someone's installed the app, he can only listen to the song if no one else is listening to it. If it's not available, he'll be put in a queue and notified when it becomes available. When he receives the message, he has one hour in which to listen to the song, after which the opportunity will be passed on the next person in line. I'm still waiting to listen to it—but waiting for Adam's new single meant that I was thinking about him more, which made me want to listen to some of his old stuff.

Facebook friends, Twitter followers, LinkedIn connections—the sum total of a person's social media connections signal his or her status. If you can find a way to reward that status, you'll have a great giving campaign.

Sponsorship

Sponsorship is one of the oldest and purest forms of giving; unfortunately, it has lost its way. In the traditional sense, sponsorship is about a company making something that other people enjoy possible; there couldn't be a more obvious way to make a deposit. There's a reason that sponsorship has lost its character: In the past 20 years or so, it's become less about actually making something happen and more about slapping your logo on an event you're sponsoring in order to increase your sales. But the transparency of the social era and people's increasing marketing savvy mean that they see right through such tactics, turning the sponsorship from a deposit into a withdrawal.

When I worked at MTV, finding sponsors for our main awards shows, such as the MTV Europe Music Awards, was essential for our survival. But to my astonishment, many sponsors didn't care about the show, didn't care about the music, and didn't care about the young people enjoying the music. Their main concern was to make sure that their sales increased. We never heard sponsors ask "How can we make the visitor experience better? How can we improve the viewing experience for people at home? How can we ensure that the artists will love performing on our stage?"—all forms of genuine giving. Just imagine how much it would be worth if you could succeed in genuinely giving something to Beyoncé on a night like that and have her turn into a fan of your brand. Incredible! But no—the only questions the sponsors asked were: "Can Beyoncé hold one of our products during her performance? How many times can we air our new ad during the show? Can the presenter say something about our new product on the show?" The Mentos brand manager at the time even asked if Beyoncé could have a Mentos during her performance! ("Excuse me—do you mean while she's *singing*?") All of these requests take away from the show itself—they're withdrawals. People notice this; you don't even have to be very marketing-savvy to see through these brands' pretense to their true intention.

So when delving into sponsorship, do what needs to be done: choose a clear mission that's close to your product. Take Wimbledon, for example. The tennis tournament boasts a bunch of great brands that have been committed to it for a very long time: Slazenger and Wimbledon have been partners for 110 years; Robinsons and Wimbledon for 75 years; and Rolex and Wimbledon for 30 years. At the tournament, you'll see absolutely no board sponsorship; in fact, it *looks* entirely sponsor-free. The sponsors (visibly) do what they do best: Slazenger provides the tennis balls, Robinsons supplies the drinks—Robinson's bottles are available and visible on the umpires' chairs—and Rolex is the official timekeeper, so its clocks are used on court. All of the sponsors' products serve a purpose at the tournament and appear exactly where people *expect* to see them. That the link is logical helps the brands show what they are capable of and at the same time build a brand connection to one of the world's most prestigious sporting tournaments.

Apps and games

An app or a game is way to get actively involved with a brand. The spectrum here is very broad; you can entertain, inspire, or challenge people. When done well, it can be a real deposit. Unfortunately, as I said in Chapter 1, 80% of all branded apps are downloaded fewer than 1,000 times. What goes for any giving marketing activation is as true—or even more so—for an app. To cut through the humongous clutter of a major app store, you have to make sure that the app or game itself not only builds the brand and product, but also has value itself. People need to *want* the app or game.

An example of a great giving app was one that the cosmetics company Nivea created in Brazil. Nivea's challenge was to strengthen its customers' relationship with the brand, and it decided to meet that challenge by offering them a great new service.

Have you ever planned to get up early to go to the beach, only to awake in the middle of a downpour? To make sure that this never happens again, Nivea created a mobile app perfect for all beachgoers and sun lovers: the alarm time is set just like on a regular alarm clock—but the alarm only goes off if the sun is out. The Sun Alarm is connected to a weather channel and updates weather conditions in real time. If the weather's bad, the alarm doesn't ring and people can keep sleeping. So: it's an alarm clock that only gets Brazilians out of bed if it's a sunny morning—something that's especially useful in the country's changeable tropical climate. And the numbers show that Brazilians found it useful: the app stayed in first place for a few weeks at the Brazilian affiliate of the Apple App Store and is a huge success at Google Play. In total, the app has already been downloaded more than 100,000 times.

This app ticks all of the boxes for me. It's clearly linked to the brand and product: "Wake up, it's sunny out! Put your sunscreen on and head to the beach!" On top of that, it's something truly valuable and giving. Imagine how someone will feel when she wakes up naturally at 10 a.m. instead of the 8 a.m. she set as her alarm time: disappointment because of the lack of sun, but satisfaction at being able to sleep a little longer—and all thanks to Nivea. (Who doesn't love a little extra sleep?) Third, it shows that, if you use some creativity, it's still possible to create something unique and fun that will differentiate your brand.

Social media

In my eyes, social media is a giving form of marketing in principle, because people choose whether they want to like, follow, and listen to a brand. And if they stop liking the brand, it's very easy to unfollow or unfriend it. Although this book is called *The Social Brand*, it's not primarily about social *media*, but about how your *brand* has to be social in order to be successful in this day and age.

Placing an ad on a social media platform naturally falls into the withdrawal category. It's difficult for brands to turn a social media friend or follower into an actual brand lover. Too many brands take an approach that's exactly backwards. They start by getting as many Facebook friends or Twitter followers as possible, and only *then* do they start asking themselves what they're going to tell those people. One company that understands social media really well is KLM. The Dutch airline has received a number of prizes and gotten a lot of positive PR for its approach to social media. One of the great elements of this approach is the amount of transparency and vulnerability it shows. KLM's social media hub has a blog where the airline publicly posts about its strategy. For example:

> *Back in the summer of 2009, a small group of department representatives gathered each week to discuss the rise of social networks and how they related to KLM. Rather than blindly setting up accounts, thinking "We have to do something with social media", we took the time to observe, listen, and learn. We noticed how travelers were exchanging experiences with each other, how the media were listening in, and how online sentiment was having an increasing impact on consumer choices and brand reputations. We concluded that, by becoming an active part of the online dialogue, we could increase brand engagement, strengthen our reputation, and ultimately sell more*

tickets. It was in these early days that we created the solid base that is now one of the keys to our success: cooperation.

Now, 50 staff members devoted to social media offer an authentic, open dialogue in Dutch, English, Spanish, German, and Japanese 24 hours a day and handle more than 2,000 conversations each week with the airline's two million Facebook friends.

Two aspects of the KLM case show that the airline really gets it. The first element is *what* it decided to do with social media. KLM did not ask itself the question "What are we going to *say* to people?" Instead, it decided to *listen*, which is a key trait of a Social Brand. KLM simply decided to answer questions people had about the primary service the airline offers: flying people from one place to another. KLM used social media to answer questions like "Is my flight delayed?" and "Where can I find the cheapest tickets?" But not only does it answer the day-to day questions, but every now and then, it seizes a great opportunity that comes along. For example, a passenger who tweeted that he was going to miss his football team's match due to being in New York was presented with a *Lonely Planet New York City* guide by a KLM stewardess with all the best sports bars in the city highlighted. That *Lonely Planet* probably retailed for $20, but the value to the football fan was immeasurable. Perhaps the most colorful example came in 2012 when, in response to a tweet lamenting the lack of direct flights between Amsterdam and Miami during the Ultra Music Festival, KLM put a challenge to its Twitter followers: fill a plane and we'll fly you to the party. In just five hours, the airline had filled a jumbo jet with fully paid-up passengers. Simply by listening and responding, KLM transformed one man's disappointment into a marketing campaign that brought the brand's commitment to its customers to life in the most vibrant of ways. These are not one-off media stunts—these are a result of the airline's long-term commitment to listening.

Your own digital or social platform

Hosting your own web domain or page on a social channel like Facebook is in principle a deposit in the same way that a brand or concept store is; you choose to visit it or like it. What you decide to do with it can, of course, still sway it in one direction or another. A great example of a giving web platform is movember.com and the Movember page on Facebook.

If you haven't heard of it, Movember—a combination of the words "moustache" and "November"—is an annual event that urges men to grow moustaches during the month of November to raise awareness of men's health issues like prostate cancer and the charities that support those issues. The goal of Movember is "to change the face of men's health". Started in 2004 in Australia and New Zealand, Movember has grown to become a nearly global phenomenon. In 2012, *The Global Journal* first listed Movember as one of the top 100 NGOs (non-governmental organizations) in the world. According to Movember.com:

> Once registered at Movember.com, men start Movember 1st clean-shaven. For the rest of the month, these selfless and generous men, known as Mo Bros, groom, trim, and wax their way into the annals of fine moustachery. Supported by the women in

their lives, Mo Sistas, Movember Mo Bros raise funds by seeking out sponsorship for their Mo-growing efforts.

Mo Bros effectively become walking, talking billboards for the 30 days of November. Through their actions and words, they raise awareness by prompting private and public conversations around the often-ignored issue of men's health.

What's brilliant about this platform is that it has taken something very serious and made it light-hearted and fun—all based on true insight. Every man has the urge to (occasionally) grow some facial hair, and Movember provides an excellent excuse. And the "movement" is constantly evolving, getting more fun, becoming more creative, and having a larger impact. For example, the "Moscars" have been established to award prizes for the finest Mos.

There are plenty of other creative ideas swirling around to boost awareness and participation, such as real-life prizes and awards for men who grow a Mo in Movember. For instance, Byron Hamburgers was a Movember partner; men who came into a Byron restaurant sporting their Mo and showing their Movember.com registration got a free hamburger.

Internal resources and expertise

Using your company's internal resources and expertise to add value and create a giving form of marketing activation is used far too little. When done right, it can be one of the most powerful—and most brand-building—ways to give something truly valuable. Consider this example from Toyota.

After Hurricane Sandy tore through New York in October 2012, many residents relied upon relief agencies to feed their families. Eight months later, the Rockaways area of New York still required food aid as the community struggled to rebuild itself. To come to their aid, in the summer of 2013 Toyota partnered with Metro World Child, a relief agency that delivers weekly food packages to families in the Rockaways. The brand used the principles of its "Kaizen" Toyota production system—where many small improvements are made to a process in order to create a much larger overall impact—and applied these to Metro. This Japanese word, which means "continuous improvement", is one of the brand's core values and has been at the epicenter of its production line for years. According to Toyota's website, it "creates responsibility for the success of the process, increasing both morale and quality." After the blow that Toyota's Brand Bank Account took between 2009 and 2011 due to the automaker having to recall many of its cars, this again established its expertise in the most sympathetic and giving way.

Applying Toyota's Kaizen approach to the entire production chain of Metro World Child reduced the average distribution time from three hours to 70 minutes, meaning that Metro Food Distribution could feed an extra 400 families in half the time. And unlike a one-off cash donation, the relief agencies involved can employ these lessons if and when the next emergency arises. On top of this, the campaign also highlights Toyota's efficient operational processes and amplifies one of the brand's most important values—Kaizen.

Content

Content. I'll end with this one. Why? Because everything I've said above are the things you do to create content. Very often—in fact, nearly always—people ask me how to create good content. But again, that's the wrong question to ask. You should start by asking: "What am I going to *do* for the people who matter for me? What will they value?" Only once you've answered those questions should you ask how to create content that is compelling and will spread.

The number-one ingredient of success is storytelling. At MTV and Red Bull, we were relentless when it came to telling a story—and doing so in a single easy sentence. (My team at Red Bull probably got very sick of me always asking "What's the one-liner? What's the message?") What was the difference between Red Bull Stratos (which the whole world watched) and the executive from Google jumping from space (which no one noticed)? Storytelling.

I could write an entire book on storytelling, but here's the nickel version. A good story has three building blocks: first—and foremost—find something you want to *do* for the people who matter to you; only then find the best medium to tell that story; and finally make sure that story can be explained in a crisp and compelling tweet. When you mention "content", most people think of moving image (film)—but it can be everything from spoken word to photography to live events to podcasts; content can be brought to life through just about any medium.

Content is obviously a form of giving because it's something that someone personally and actively decides to engage with, regardless of whether that content is on TV, on a brand's website, or on a third-party website like YouTube. As we've already discussed, the exact same rules apply to "branded" content as to "normal" content: the better it is, the more people will watch it. Again, this sounds rather straightforward—but so many brands have still not gotten this right; they focus too much on putting their product at the center of the content. At the very least, they're not asking themselves the question that producers of "normal" content ask themselves every day: "What makes good content?" As with all forms of giving marketing, you should think of content as a product in its own right. Products actually give something of value. Products help establish a company's mission. Ask yourself the product questions again: is it new, relevant, transparent, and easy to communicate? Does it deliver?

A great giving example is the WestJet Christmas Miracle, which occurred a couple of weeks before Christmas 2013. When passengers checking in at Toronto's Pearson and Hamilton airports for flights to Calgary scanned their boarding passes at airline kiosks, they were asked by a virtual Santa what they wanted for Christmas. Responses ranged from underwear and socks to tablet computers and flatscreen TVs.

What the 250 passengers didn't know is that, during the five hours they were in the air, a team of more than 150 WestJet staff bought the gifts the passengers had wished for, wrapped them, and delivered them to the Calgary airport. When the unsuspecting passengers landed and went to collect their luggage, they saw wrapped presents—including the big-screen TV!—addressed to them coming down the carousel. Naturally, a camera crew was on hand to record passengers' reactions. WestJet, which began mapping out the project in August, had hoped that the video would go viral and pledged that once the video reached 200,000 views, it would donate free flights to Ronald McDonald House Charities. The video hit one million YouTube views the same day it was posted; a week later, at the end of 2013, it had nearly 35 million.

This, for me, ticks all the boxes; it's a genuinely surprising and giving idea. And the fact that WestJet staff carried out the project themselves made it a highly motivational event for the airline as well. At the same time, WestJet made sure to create real emotional content—you simply can't watch the video without a tear coming to your eye. So rather than commissioning a traditional ad and buying a lot of media, the airline bought Christmas presents for its customers instead and in so doing created a great piece of content that went out and spread itself.

If you decide to go down the road of moving image content, it's important to be aware of who you commission to produce it for you; this is probably the hardest—and most expensive—nut to crack. You have a number of options, ranging from doing it in-house to letting your advertising agency have a go at it. If you don't yet have loads of experience as a brand or as a business, you would be best served by going one of two routes. You could go to a content producer that has its own platform, such as Vice Media, MTV, Give Me Sport, or Big Balls Films—or you could take a look at professional dedicated content producers like Caperock.tv, which makes content for a living but is also savvy when it comes to spreading that content. As everyone will tell you, you have to tailor your content to the platform, whether that's a six-second Vine video or a 52-minute long-form piece on TV.

Summary and critical question

Summary

The first thing you give people is your product; in exchange, you ask them to pay a certain price. Then you add a brand that enhances the product's value. You promote this product and brand with forms of marketing that can either give or take. Giving forms of marketing are more effective to help you build a Social Brand, but that doesn't mean that you should never use a taking form of marketing; sometimes you just need the reach and awareness that only TV or radio can deliver. The most important thing is that you know how many deposits and how many withdrawals you're making and where the balance between them lies. It's not called a *balance* for nothing; make sure your Brand Bank Account is balanced by giving more than you take.

Critical question

Fill in a Brand Bank Account balance sheet. List all of the forms of marketing you use and put them on either the left or right side of the sheet, depending on whether they're giving or taking forms of marketing. Most importantly, put the *budget* you spend on each of these marketing activities onto the balance sheet; in particular, make sure that you also put all of the money you spend on producing the taking form of media on the withdrawals side. So if you spend $500,000 to make a TV spot and $2 million to air it, that's $2.5 million in withdrawals. When you measure your efforts in financial terms, do you give more or take more? Be honest, now!

CHAPTER EIGHT

How to reach many people with giving marketing

People can't buy from you if they don't know you.

We're getting close to the end of the book, and all the theory on how to create a Social Brand and promote that brand with giving marketing activations has now been laid out before you. Due to the nature of giving marketing (making deposits), it can be more difficult to generate the key elements of marketing: reaching a large group of people, controlling who you reach and where and when you do so. Naturally, it's more difficult to reach a large number of people when you set out to give—to actually *do* something *for* people—than when you simply *tell* them about your brand. However, awareness is, and will remain, essential for success.

Awareness

If people don't know you exist, they won't buy from you. It may sound obvious, but many current marketing books—especially those that focus on social media—seem to have forgotten this basic fact. You could have a great product, a fabulous Social Brand—but people have to know about it or it won't go anywhere. Bill Gates' famous maxim that "content is king" sounds great, but I guarantee that there's plenty of magnificent content out there in the world (wide web) that nobody has ever seen. Rupert Murdoch took it even further, saying that content is not just "king", but "emperor". Then again, he owns all of the channels and products that have the power to push that content right into your face! New and interesting start-ups, brand extensions, and fun stores pop up every day. Lots of people have great ideas—but in order to succeed, you have to find a way to become known.

When launching a new product, getting the product basics right is an important first step. Making sure that your product meets the five requirements of a good product in the social era (discussed in Chapter 4) will definitely help drive awareness even in the absence of any marketing money. To repeat Jeff Bezos' great quote: "Advertising is the price you pay for having an unremarkable product or service." David Taylor says this well in his book *The Brand Gym*: "Usain Bolt is the fastest man on earth, winning gold at the Olympics twice; but who got the bronze? We all know who Barack Obama is; but who was his running mate?" The number-ones get all the attention, so if you're really at the top of a category—or, preferably, if you've *created* the category—people will remember you.

Committing to becoming a social brand

Whether you're a new brand looking for a way to become known or an established brand keen to move away from being a positioned brand, you have to commit to becoming a Social

Brand. If you're an established player in the market, but you realize that you're currently spending most of your money on traditional *taking* media and have decided that you want to start *giving*, you unfortunately can't use a full-fledged advertising campaign that explains that "We're now more giving." It's not as easy as it was in the days of repositioning; the foundation of a Social Brand is actually giving—not just telling people that you're giving. The only way forward is by *being* different and *doing* different things, not by *saying* that you're different. At the same time, especially if you're a big brand, you can't start doing something for everyone who already buys your brand *and* all of your potential buyers; that's simply too many people to try to reach.

To get a good feel for the task at hand, compare your brand with a person. To really drive the point home, picture the most annoying (taking) person you've ever known. Let's say it's a high-school classmate named Jack who's been bullying you every day for years. If Jack comes to school one day and starts telling everybody that he has changed—that he's become a really nice guy—nobody will believe him. And the louder and more often he screams about this, the less likely you'll be to believe him. But, you think, maybe he *has* changed. If that's true, there are four ways for Jack to demonstrate to people that the change is real. First, and most powerfully, he could actually do something nice for you. For example, some of Jack's old friends are picking on you after school, and Jack comes along and tells his old friends to behave and bugger off. Now *that's* a deposit you will never forget! And that is the fundamental principle underlying this book: *go out and do something worthwhile for people.*

But, as I mentioned before, when you're a large brand, it's not always possible to personally do something for everyone. To return to our example, even though Jack has changed his behavior, it's a very large school; no matter how nice Jack has become, he can't protect everyone from his former bully friends—and you worry that he might revert to being a bully. No worries! The second powerful way to become convinced of Jack's new image is to discover for yourself that he has changed. For instance, you see him help an old lady cross the road when he believes no one is watching. This is something he never would have done previously. But now you've seen it with your own eyes: his actions match his intentions. The third powerful way to change your perception of Jack is if someone else you trust tells you that he saw Jack help an old lady cross the road when nobody was watching. People may not perceive Jack differently the first time he does, but he *has* made his first deposit. If you start seeing more of this on a regular basis, you might actually start to *like* Jack! The fourth and last way is for Jack to tell people he's actually changed—and then convince them that it is so.

Making your deposits known

There are thus four ways to help people find out that your brand has made a deposit:

- **Make the deposit!** Do something worthwhile for someone.
- **Self-discovery.** People discover for themselves that you've made a deposit.
- **Word of mouth.** People hear about your deposits from their friends, whether offline or via one of the many online variations (tweets, shares, likes, etc.).

- **Advertising.** People find out that you've given something via advertising that you create; preferably, these ads will use actual footage of the deposits.

The higher up in the list, the more engaging and credible the deposit is; the lower down, the more potential there is for greater reach and awareness. It's very important to realize that the first three aren't just a matter of luck; they require planning, creativity, and commitment. Your deposit won't just go viral on its own! I've already discussed (in Chapter 7) the different forms that deposits can take; in this chapter, I'll discuss the three ways for people to find out that you've made one.

Self-discovery

We live in a time where every little piece of the world and nearly everything that lives on it have been discovered. Sure, there are some species of flora and fauna that we have yet to encounter, but the chances that you or I will do that are pretty slim. Yet discovering new things is still one of life's greatest pleasures. That's why it's great to be a kid! My 2½-year-old son's favorite thing is to point at something he's never seen before and say: "What-a-that-now?" When we go to see the elephants at the zoo, he's just as surprised to see a duck swimming in the pond in front of the elephants: "Hey! That-a-now?" Unfortunately, we're no longer kids and don't live in a time when we can be a Captain Cook or a Jacques Cousteau. Yet we still love discovery. So what do we discover now? It can be anything: new products, new brands, new items of clothing, new books, or new bits of online content. And it feels more special when you discover something yourself; when you stumble upon a new band while surfing the Internet or browsing YouTube, it means more than if a friend recommended it to you or you saw an ad for the band's new album.

While I was writing this book, I was on a five-month sabbatical with my family—my wonderful wife Cindy and our adorably 2½-year-old twins. New Zealand was one of our destinations, and Abel Tasman Park on the north end of the south island was one of the highlights of the trip for me. Once we arrived at the park in our camper, we put the kids to bed early (when you travel with small children, it's both pleasant and necessary to set aside some "me time" every now and then). Someone had told me that the tide was exceptionally low that evening, so I told my wife that I was going for a stroll on the beach, even though it was raining a little.

The tide indeed seemed very low; it had ebbed by a couple of kilometers. It felt like I was walking on the bottom of the ocean. From my vantage point on the shore, where the beach met the forest, I saw something small and white a couple of kilometers away. I had no idea what it was, but somehow it drew me in. Even though it was getting darker—the sun had already gone behind the mountains, which were wreathed in clouds—I started walking toward the object. I had to take my shoes off and wade through some pretty high water to get there. Halfway there, the clouds dissolved, a rainbow appeared, and the sky glowed the most beautiful shades of pink, red, and purple. It was breathtaking. I was getting closer and closer to my goal, but because of the dusk I still couldn't clearly make out what it was that was attracting me so. All I knew was that I wanted to get there.

After a good hour and a half of walking and wading, I finally reached my goal. Tears came to my eyes. It was a beautiful cone-shaped rock on top of which—and this seemed hardly possible—grew a small tree. It was one of the most beautiful things I had ever seen. It was my own personal discovery! Convinced that the rock under this tree had for the very first time revealed itself to the human eye because of the exceptionally low tide, I decided to name the spot after my wife and dubbed it "Cindy's Cone-Rock Tree".

Two hours later, I had just barely made it back to the camper. It was pitch-black and raining hard, the tide was coming back in, and my feet were bloody from walking on shells. But I was still ecstatic. I told my wife that I had just discovered this beautiful little tree on top of a white cone-shaped rock and had named it after her!

The next day we took the boat from that very same beach to head deeper into Abel Tasman Park. The first site they showed us was "Split Apple Rock", which featured in all of the brochures about the region. I didn't think it was half as nice as "Cindy's Cone-Rock Tree". As we went further, to my surprise I saw that we were going to pass my discovery. I was wondering what the rest of the boat was going to think of the little tree and what our guide would say about it. We passed the spot (only the tree was visible; the rock was under water), the guide said nothing, no one noticed, and Cindy was slightly disappointed. After my ecstatic story, she had expected a little more. And I had to admit that I understood why "Split Apple Rock" had made the brochure and "Cindy's Cone-Rock Tree" had not.

This self-discovery story is just as true for new brands, new products, and new marketing activities. When people discover something themselves, they rate it more highly; it's more convincing and credible. And, very importantly, makes it more likely that they will share it with their friends.

Word of mouth

A great method of finding out about a brand's deposit is through word of mouth (WOM). A lot has been said and written on the subject; people are more likely to believe something positive about a brand if someone they trust tells them than if the brand delivers the message itself. What makes this powerful is that it works even if people *don't know* the person giving this advice. I found many of the hotels and campgrounds that I booked during my sabbatical on the TripAdvisor website, so the choices I made were solely based on the recommendations of people I didn't know. Of course, I won't trust a hotel with only one great recommendation; my skeptical human nature tells me that this review is probably the owner recommending his own place under a false name. But once there are 20 or more people saying that it's the best place they've ever stayed in, and if it's within my price range, I book a room immediately.

A great (and already famous) recent example of WOM is the launch of The Wizarding World of Harry Potter theme park in Florida. The vice president of new media and marketing partnerships at Universal Orlando Resort, Cindy Gordon, had the responsibility of planning a marketing strategy to introduce the theme park. With the huge budget she was given, she could have chosen any type of media or form of marketing platform that her heart desired. What she actually chose to do was to tell just *seven people* about it. She chose these people from the most popular Harry Potter fan sites and announced the theme park to them during a secret midnight webcast. You can probably already guess where this story's going! Right after the webcast, all seven people blogged about the announcement. Lots of their followers then also blogged about it and talked it up on social media—and the ball just kept rolling. Eventually, the mainstream media got wind of it and started to write about it. Within 24 hours of telling seven people about the new theme park, 350 million people had heard about it. OK, so you probably don't have something as hot as Harry Potter in your pipeline. But the idea is still the same: find something of value that is truly a deposit for some people. They'll go out and spread the word for you.

In the social era, it's easy to labor under the misconception that all things "social" take place online. But according to a recent study by InSites Consulting, only 10% of our social interactions are online interactions; the rest are just old-fashioned "real-life" connections. You could argue that many of the other 90% of social interactions involve people talking about the 10% they saw online—but no matter how you see it, it's vital to find out how shareable and discussable your product, brand, and marketing activation are. So you have to make sure that you have a quality marketing activation that people want to share and promote—*and* that the quality activation reaches the right people with the right influence.

Even though the concept of WOM has been around for many years in marketing, I think people still severely underestimate its power—mostly because it's very difficult to measure. Determining the ROI of WOM is *hard*—so people don't use it enough. But the whole theory of a Brand Bank Account is based on making a difference, whether that's to one person or to many people. If you do something worthwhile for people, they will surely tell others.

Advertising

Advertising is, of course, still either a withdrawal (TV and online advertising like pre-rolls) or neutral (cinema, print, and outdoor), but sometimes it's necessary to reach a large amount of people at the time and place you need to reach them.

In Chapter 4, we discussed how key it is to be transparent about your product and marketing activation. One area that still lags far behind in terms of transparency: advertising. Ad agencies, directors, and actors create worlds designed to give you a certain impression of a brand—and it's easy for their collective creative vision to take liberties with the truth.

And every now and then, brands go too far—like what happened with the ad accompanying the launch of the Nokia Lumia 920, the handset manufacturer's flagship smartphone. The ad showed a man using the Lumia to film his girlfriend while both of them were riding bicycles. The ad cut from professionally filmed footage of both actors to video that Nokia claimed was filmed with the man's Lumia. A split-screen sequence then compared what the smartphone footage would look like with Nokia's optical image stabilization feature turned on and switched off. So far, so good. But then they ride past a window, and in the reflection coming off of the window you can clearly see that first of all, the man isn't on a wobbly bike, but in a big steady van; second of all, he's not even using the phone to do the filming.

When the tech site The Verge exposed this deception, Nokia was publicly humiliated and its stock price took a hit. But, in my eyes, the worst was yet to come. When Nokia was confronted with these embarrassing facts, it only made things worse for itself; it apologized, *but* then only said that it should have "posted a disclaimer". (WHAT?!?!?!?) What the company *should* have said, but didn't: "Sorry, we should have just filmed it on our brand-new Lumia 920 smartphone." But apparently, the phone's video capture wasn't all that great to start with.

More and more, I believe that people will no longer accept advertising that just tries to create a great world filled with happy actors using such and such a brand. People will demand that your brand do real things, whether that's a true representation of the product you sell or an actual giving activation that you've fulfilled. For instance, look at what Google Maps did. To emphasize that Google is serious about its quest to "map the world", it sent a team of ten people and five cameras off road for three days to explore 75 miles of trails and roads in the spectacular terrain of the Grand Canyon. The Google Maps team trekked on foot around the rocky terrain with the Android-operated Trekker, a wearable 15-lens camera system, mounted on their backpacks. The team created more than 9,500 panoramas of the Grand Canyon, all of which can be viewed on Google Maps; it's pretty impressive to see these sights from the comfort of your desk. You can view them all online, but Google also created an ad about the quest, showing what the team actually *did*. A month after the video was posted on YouTube, it had already been watched 1.5 million times.

Getting the message out to the right people

So: the tools you have at your disposal to spread your marketing activation are self-discovery, WOM, and advertising. I don't say "tools" for nothing in this context, because many times marketers simply expect their activations to "just go viral". But discovery and WOM, just like advertising, require planning, creativity, and budget. It starts by making sure that you create something that's worth sharing. Let's have a look at how to measure that.

Promoters

First, it's important to find out whether you've created something worth sharing. In 2003, Fred Reichheld introduced the concept of the "Net Promoter Score" (NPS) in the *Harvard Business Review*. NPS is obtained by asking people to respond to a single question ("How likely is it that you would recommend our company to a friend or colleague?") on a scale from 0 to 10. The responses are then put into three groups: Promoters (everyone giving a score of 9 or 10), Passives (scores of 7 or 8), and Detractors (scores from 0 to 6). The percentage of Detractors is then subtracted from the percentage of Promoters to obtain the NPS.

One caveat: NPS is not used to measure WOM; it's intended to measure loyalty. A number of research specialists dispute NPS's effectiveness, saying that it's no better than traditional ways of measuring loyalty. But I believe that NPS can be used as a tool to measure your *potential* WOM. If somebody is a Promoter, he may not be *loyal* to the brand (something that skeptics criticize about NPS), but there's no denying that he will *promote* it. I also don't think that it's necessary to subtract the Detractors; discussion between Promoters and Detractors is a great way to get people talking about your brand. The "Apple *vs.* all other computers" debate has certainly done Apple no harm, no matter how passionate its detractors may be.

So it's easy and cheap to find out if people are promoting your brand, product, or marketing activation. Find some people important to your brand, show them what you'd like to bring to market, and use a short, simple online questionnaire to ask them if they would promote it or not. Or as Reichheld recommends, ask them how *likely* it is that they would promote it and count everyone who responds with a 9 or 10 as Promoters.

Three degrees of influence

Now that you know that you've created something worth sharing, the next important questions are: What is that worth? How many people will they promote it to? How many people will they be able to influence? In their book *Connected,* Harvard professors Nicholas Christakis and James Fowler show how this could work and how much influence one person can have in their network. Christakis and Fowler used the "six degrees of separation" theory masterminded by Stanley Milgram as their starting point. Many of you will have heard of Milgram's theory, which shows that people are all connected to one another by an average of six degrees of separation (your friend is one degree away from you, your friend's friend is two degrees away, and so on).

Christakis and Fowler wondered how far one person's influence extends over the distance of these six degrees: can you influence someone six steps away from you? Their research found that a person can, on average, influence the first three of the six degrees. Naturally, they called this the "three degrees of influence rule". *Everything* (!!) people do or say tends to ripple through their network, having an impact on their friends (one degree), their friends' friends (two degrees), and even their friends' friends' friends (three degrees). After that point, most people have no noticeable influence. Christakis and Fowler indicated that their rule applies to a broad range of attitudes, feelings, and behaviors and applies to the spread of phenomena as diverse as political views, weight loss or gain, happiness, and mundane domestic topics like finding a piano teacher or a good home for a pet. They concluded that the effect we have on each other is extraordinary.

Let's say that you have 20 social contacts, each of which has the same number of contacts (to make things simple, let's assume that their contacts are different from yours). According to Christakis and Fowler, then, if you manage to influence one person, you're actually influencing $20 \times 20 \times 20 = 8,000$ people! And as they clearly state, this is your *everyday* influence—they're not even talking about the kind of things you actively *want* to go out and promote (things that you would rate a 9 or 10 on the NPS scale). The 8,000 score could even be higher if you look at the number of people you can reach on Facebook and Twitter: consider that the average person on Facebook has about 130 friends and about the same number follow the average Twitter account.

The British anthropologist Robin Dunbar has a theory that backs this up. There is a theoretical limit to the number of people with whom we can maintain a stable social relationship. According to Dunbar, this number is somewhere between 100 and 230, with a commonly used value of 150. This is pretty close to the number of Facebook friends and Twitter followers most people have! Thus, science (Dunbar) and facts on the ground (Facebook and Twitter) tell us that 130 is about the number of people one person can influence to promote a brand, product, or marketing activity that has done something truly worthwhile for that person. Combining that number with the three degrees of influence means that by influencing one person, you could reach 130×130×130 (more than two million people!) with that brand, product, or message.

The power of influence

If you look at the three degrees of influence, you can figure out how shareable your marketing activation is and how many people you could potentially reach. Once you've done that, you can start laying out your strategy. If you go down the advertising route, this is "easy": nothing's changed from your old ways of doing things—just pick up the phone and call your media agency. But you can also plan how you will facilitate self-discovery and WOM. If you want your activation to be discovered, you have to get it out there; traditionally, this means getting it into the press by making journalists enthusiastic about whatever it is that you've created. As David Meerman Scott rightly points out in his book *The New Rules of Marketing & PR*, "Think and act like a publisher!" This doesn't only apply to the "old media" of TV, radio, newspapers, and magazines; there is now a wide range of influencers who are not journalists per se.

Klout is an analytics company that measures the influence of people who use various forms of social media, mainly Facebook, Twitter, and LinkedIn. The company itself says:

Klout measures your influence based on your ability to drive action on social networks. We crunch your social data to give you insight into how influential you are and what you are influential about. Inspiring your friends to talk about and try a new sushi bar down the street after you post a photo of the incredible sushi you had is an example of influence. We believe everyone has influence. The more engagement and action you inspire with the content you create, the greater your influence.

You have the opportunity to influence people anywhere you have an online presence by creating or sharing content that inspires actions such as likes, retweets, and comments. The more engagement your posts receive, the more influential you are. Klout uses this information to calculate a "Klout score" that measures your overall influence. The company tries to keep the exact algorithm of calculating someone's Klout score a secret, fearing that people will try to unfairly boost their score (everyone likes to have power and influence!).

As you might guess, President Obama has the world's highest Klout score of 99 points, followed closely by (yes, really!) Justin Bieber at 92. Although several researchers have called the accuracy of Klout scores into question—often by observing that *online* influence is distinct from *true* influence—the principle of people having measurable and different Klout scores seems obvious.

If your brand has a Twitter account with a bunch of followers, you can attach a Klout score to every follower you have, see which of your responders and retweeters have the most Klout, and move forward accordingly. This is becoming more and more commonplace; for example, fashion designer Carolina Herrera threw a party that you could only go to if you had a certain number of Facebook friends. Klout and PeerIndex (a platform that offers similar technology and services) both give select people exclusive deals to reward their social status.

Klout is one way of looking at influence, but there are many ways to see if someone is influential. Where Klout measures broad influence on any topic using the major social platforms, there are many more specialist influencers that can be far more powerful within their (and perhaps your) field. Take, for instance, the travel industry, where TripAdvisor has become a major influencer due to the millions of contributors to its site. The more you contribute, the higher your contributor level (there are five possible levels). And the higher your level or the more your contribution is liked, the higher up it will be when people are checking out a hotel or B&B—making your review the first thing people see when they're considering where to stay. Top contributors thus have huge influence. When someone books a hotel, the owner can check whether his new guest is very active on TripAdvisor and treat her accordingly. My wife, an avid traveler and TripAdvisor contributor, has achieved the highest level possible on the platform. We've had many upgrades, free welcome drinks, and spontaneous breakfasts in bed ever since. I'm pretty sure that's no coincidence.

If you want your marketing activation to spread, you have to find the influencers in your category. This sounds a bit tougher than the old-fashioned "buy media that target the people you want to reach." But it is possible—and, given the many online tools and agencies, there are plenty of ways to do it.

Klout and TripAdvisor show that, more and more, the power is with the people. So it's no longer about pulling a media stunt or trying to influence the press; anyone can be an influencer for your brand. On one hand, it's important to try to find out who the influencers are; on the other, it's simply about treating all of your customers with care and respect and making deposits. Give people something truly worthwhile and they will do your marketing for you. Not only is it free, it's much more genuine—and thus more effective.

Summary and critical question

Summary

In order to be successful, your brand has to be known. It's more difficult to reach a large number of people when you set out to give than when you simply *tell* them about something about your brand. There are three ways or levels for people to experience or find out that you've made a deposit:

- **Self-discovery.** People discover for themselves that you've made a deposit to someone else.
- **Word of mouth.** People have heard about your deposits from their friends, whether offline or via one of the many online variations (tweets, shares, likes, etc.).
- **Advertising.** People find out that you've given something via advertising that you create that uses actual content of the deposits.

The higher up in the list, the more engaging and credible the deposit is; the lower down, the more potential there is for greater reach and awareness. It's important to emphasize that deposits don't "just go viral"; it takes planning, creativity, and budget. But the basic principles always remain the same:

- Your deposit must be something people are truly enthusiastic about and keen to share.
- Know who will most influence your brand and your specific deposit/marketing activation. Once you know who the influencers are, find a way to reach them.

Critical question

Do you know who the most important influencers of your brand and your most-used marketing activations are? Make an effort to find them, treat them well, and keep them on board. They're a priceless asset.

CHAPTER NINE

Inspiring examples of giving marketing

Leaders don't create the trend—the first followers do.

There's nothing more inspiring than looking at brands that seem to have covered all the bases. Before I go into a couple of examples, I'd like to summarize what a Social Brand is. To see if the brands I'm about to mention actually check all of the boxes, let's take one last look at what boxes need to be checked.

Super-short summary

To create a Social Brand:
1. Make sure the product:
   a. Really is something new and unique (it must differentiate).
   b. Is relevant.
   c. Delivers on its promises.
   d. Is transparent.
   e. Is easy to convey (can you tell it in a tweet?).

2. Have a clear brand mission. The brand mission is a clear role based on a true insight. You don't (just) communicate about this mission; you actually go out and take it. Fulfill your mission, and do so with a consistent and authentic personality based on the purpose of your product.

3. Add the extra 20% by linking the brand mission to the product. The brand mission and marketing communications must clearly build and convey the most important product benefit(s).

4. Use the right media mix. Balance the taking and giving forms of media. Make sure that your Brand Bank Account maintains a positive balance.

So, with that out of the way, let's take a look at some great examples of giving marketing—of real deposits. I'll use examples from different industries (electronics, telecommunications, and sporting goods) to show that it's possible to give in any market segment and finish up with a fourth example: a start-up in a service industry.

Apple

Apple's main source of awareness and brand building is, of course, its products—and they're all out there to give. It shows in the mission that the company was founded on: make computers available and easy to use for everyone!

Apple balances its marketing mix very nicely, hardly if ever using really taking forms of advertising. Very rarely do you see Apple TV ads broadcast on a global scale; when the company's done so in the past, it was usually in a context like the Super Bowl (we all remember the ad that introduced the Macintosh in 1984!). Apple tends to use "neutral" outdoor ads to get the awareness it needs for its products—ads that employ simple photographs of how (good) the products look and what you can do with them.

On top of that, Apple has all kinds of great deposits. The brand's retail stores are another perfect example of giving marketing. Apple doesn't simply *tell* you to "think different" or "be creative" in ad campaigns; it actually supports you in doing so—just like a good Social Brand should. Take the Apple Store on Fifth Avenue in Manhattan. It runs about six workshops a day—on the house. The more basic workshops cover how to use Apple products in a more creative and effective way, but the store also offers in-depth courses in the form of Pro Labs. During these eight-hour, four-part courses—again, free of charge—people will meet fellow aspiring creative professionals and learn solution-based workflows from Apple's team of expert trainers. Creative types can find courses on Aperture (professional photography), Final Cut Pro (editing), and Logic Pro (writing, recording, and editing your own music). Small businesses wanting to get bigger can use Apple's free workshops to get help with creating business presentations, videos, websites, and brochures.

It's not just practical stuff; Apple has always been about inspiration. Some recent (free) workshops and presentations held at the Regent Street store in London featured Colin Firth on his Oscar-winning role in the movie *The King's Speech*; Marcus Chown, author of *The Solar System* and runner-up for the Royal Society Winton Prize for Science Books; and comedian Jimmy

Carr. There's no doubt in my mind that if you visit one of these workshops—whether to improve your iPhoto skills or chat with Colin Firth—you'll be a fan forever.

SingTel

Singapore Telecommunications (SingTel) is encouraging customers to donate their iPhones in a new campaign named Project Silverline. The telco is giving the refurbished handsets to members of the Lions Befrienders and Willing Hearts charities, which support vulnerable elderly Singaporeans. SingTel offers each recipient free talk time and data usage for one year. A suite of five apps that assist the elderly in their daily lives has also been preloaded onto the iPhones. The Well-Being app, for example, helps users stay healthy with exercise videos while also reminding them to take their daily medicine; the Discover app simplifies photo-taking and sharing.

In October 2012, a nationwide media campaign raised awareness and encouraged donations. The campaign included ads in the country's flagship daily paper, *The Straits Times*; Facebook ads; and point-of-purchase messaging in-store. Singapore has a rapidly aging population; according to OgilvyOne, 8% of Singaporeans are over 60, a percentage that is projected to rise to 19% by 2030. Thomas Mouritzen, managing director of OgilvyOne, said that, as a result, businesses should expect "increasing demand for senior-oriented technology solutions". It's obvious this isn't just another CSR drive, but an actual commitment to the help the elderly in Singapore get connected and stay healthy.

Nike

Nike is a brand that has always had products at its core. That's how Phil Knight started: committed to making the best shoes for athletes to enable them to perform at the highest level. These days, Nike is not only committed to the best athletes, but to "everybody who has a body". And it's no longer just about inspiration, but enablement. As Nike's Stefan Olander says, it's about shifting from products to services or adding services to products.

Indeed. Nike doesn't just communicate about what it believes in; as a real Social Brand should, the company helps people to actually go out and *Just do it!* There are so many good examples of deposits by Nike, such as the aforementioned Run London—many more than I can mention here. As the website says, "Start with a mission. Make London run." People then feel and experience this intention at the amazing Run London events Nike has organized over the years. Run London is a great way to fulfill people's desire to exercise in a social way.

Nike's latest deposit is its interactive game, NikeFuel Missions App. The game centers on the use of Nike+ products and apps like Fuelband and the Nike+ running app. It challenges users to maintain or increase their physical activity throughout the winter, when people tend to be less active. The NikeFuel Missions app features a game that imagines that the world has been conquered by extremely icy weather. Players must exercise to earn Fuel points against a timer and advance the narrative. Along the way, animated versions of Nike-sponsored athletes gave tips on how to complete missions. Everything the brand does—whether it's real life events or online tools—all have the same intention and goal: to make you run and exercise. This is clearly a social mission, and giving marketing activations make that mission happen.

Upworthy

In addition to these three well-known global brands, I also wanted to highlight Upworthy, a start-up founded on a giving idea. Upworthy is a news aggregation site that spreads stuff that matters. People are increasingly consuming their news on Facebook and Twitter, where what you get to see is decided by the meme of the day or your user history. Upworthy aims to help stories about subjects such as gay marriage, child poverty, and banking regulation compete with the Internet's obsession with cats, epic fails, and BuzzFeed. The company's mission is clearly stated on its website:

> We're a mission-driven media company. We're not a newspaper—we'd rather speak truth than appear unbiased. And we're not a political campaign—we're more interested in the powerless versus the powerful than in Democrats versus Republicans.

> But we do have a point of view. We're pro-gay marriage, and we're anti-child poverty. We think the media is horrible to women, we think climate change is real, and we think the government has a lot to learn from the Internet about efficiency, disruption, and effectiveness.

> And then there are dozens of issues where our curators disagree with each other—areas where there's legitimate debate to be

had amongst well-meaning people. We try to encourage that debate by curating great pieces of content that represent different sides.

Upworthy has already made good on the initial backing it received from investors like Chris Hughes, one of the founders of Facebook. The company now boasts at least five million daily subscribers and a website with more visitors every month than People.com, *Entertainment Weekly*, or TMZ. *Business Insider* named Upworthy "the fastest-growing media company in the world"—something investors evidently value, having rewarded the company with an additional $8 million in capital in September 2013. Co-founder Eli Pariser hopes that the business will go on to "build the most popular public-spirited media company in history."

Hughes told the *New York Times* what he believes the reason is for the company's success: "People in the media business often think they have to choose between mass appeal and substance. What I love about Upworthy—and what excites me about the significant traction they're getting—is the plan to do both at the same time. Eli and Peter have an instinctive sense of what drives people to share on the Internet." Upworthy's editorial team starts with dozens of headlines, refining them until it finds what Pariser calls "the curiosity gap"—and when someone wants to know more, they're motivated to click on something.

Just to be clear: this *is* an actual business and the founders *do* want to make money—but they want to do it while giving something of value. They're open about the fact that they make money through paid business relationships and disclose those relationships via the "Ads We Like" flag. But Upworthy says that it only makes deals "when the content itself seems meaningful to us, and when we believe it doesn't obscure the true nature of the organization that's promoting it." In this way, the company hopes to keep away from the temptation of greenwashing.

What these examples show

First of all, all four companies link the product with the brand really well, ensuring that they will build both. They can even add up to 20% more likability to their products and therefore their brands. Here's how:

- **Apple.** The company not only focuses free courses on Apple products, demonstrating all of the possibilities these products have and enabling you to be creative, it also inspires you to think differently and meet creative, like-minded people.
- **SingTel.** The telco has made its mission a true commitment: give everyone the same opportunity to stay connected. SingTel doesn't just give a couple of phones away, it makes caring for these older people shine through in the heart of everything it does—providing free mobile phones, free airtime, and custom apps to support people.
- **Nike.** Nike doesn't just say "Just do it!" (or, more recently, #makeitcount); the company is committed to really making that happen. It puts the product at the center of what it does but enhances it with services that inspire and enable people to keep going.

- **Upworthy.** For Upworthy, the content is the product. The company looks for visual content that's both meaningful and shareable and curates the things that have the best chance of going viral—inspiring people to think about and act on issues that matter.

Secondly, all of the examples have an impact on the community on many different levels. Apple inspires people to be creative; SingTel keeps the elderly connected; Nike gets you going; and Upworthy spreads content that inspires you to make a difference. I want to emphasize that the community work these companies are doing is not limited to "popular" CSR subjects like the environment or poverty—it's about making whatever impact you can on your community. (In my opinion, CSR should link what your company does best to the community, ensuring that you have the largest impact and inspiring your employees in the process.)

CHAPTER TEN

Four free marketing deposits

Give and you shall receive.

To stay true to my own theory, I thought that it would be appropriate to *give* you four examples of giving marketing. I'll show you how I'd work with different brands in different categories if they asked me to come up with marketing activations that are deposits. If you happen to work in one of these categories and like what you read, feel free to use it!

What I'll do is name the category and a brand that the marketing activity might apply to. Then I'll state one possible brand mission it could have. I'll also discuss how to check if the giving marketing activity is still close enough to the product, building that all-important extra 20%.

Brainstorm #1

Category	Home cleaning products
Possible brand	Cif
Possible brand mission	Powerfully, yet gently, clean everything people value in life, giving them the peace of mind that only a good clean house can provide.
Marketing activation	*The Cif Graffiti Team:* "If someone's sprayed graffiti on your house and no one else can help, call the C-Team."

The idea is that everyone who lives in a big city has probably been the victim of graffiti or knows people who were. For example, my house has been defaced four times; each time it took me two or three days get the graffiti off, a process that always left the façade damaged. Wouldn't it be great if you could just call the C-Team, which would clean your façade without any damage?

The great thing about this idea is that it is 100% in line with Cif's product role: strong yet gentle cleaning that completely removes the graffiti while leaving the façade intact. Removing graffiti is one of the hardest cleaning jobs there is, especially if you want to avoid damage. So if Cif can get the graffiti off of your façade, cleaning your house will be easy!

What media channels should Cif use? An online platform would be enough; word would spread quickly. Perhaps even better: a fan page on Facebook. This idea certainly has the potential for free publicity. You could even try working together with the city council; perhaps it would be willing to sponsor the C-Team.

Brainstorm #2

Category	Personal/small business banking
Possible brand	Barclays
Possible brand mission	Support people in taking that one small step to achieve what they want in life but are held back by a lack of funds, expertise, or confidence.
Marketing activation	To help start a new business or organize an existing one, Barclays provides a completely free book-keeping program; it's the best on the market and comes with no strings attached.

I'm basing this example on something that Barclays currently offers but which just doesn't go far enough to be giving. Here's how Barclays is promoting MyBusinessWorks for start-ups and small entrepreneurs:

MyBusinessWorks is a package of five applications that is only available to Barclays Business customers and covers bookkeeping, creating a business plan, secure online data backup, training courses, and all the tools you need to make sure your business is legal and compliant.

MyBusinessWorks is available to Barclays Business start-up customers for £12.50 (excluding VAT) per month from April 2011. Subscribe for 12 months and you could receive a £150 refund of Barclays Business bank charges.

To apply, speak to a Barclays Business Manager. Terms and conditions apply.

I bet that the bank thinks that this a very charitable deal. Maybe it is, but it doesn't *sound* very giving, now does it? Take a look:

- **Only available to** Barclays Business customers.
- Available for **£12.50 per month** (excluding 20% VAT, mind you!)
- Subscribe for a really long time and you **could (!) get some money back,** but only if you've paid what we've already charged you (so it doesn't cost us a thing).
- **Terms and conditions apply** (you'll probably have to remain a customer for life).

If Barclays' true mission is to support people in taking that one small step, then it should develop its own state-of-the-art bookkeeping software and give it away for free. The software should work perfectly *without* any need to do business with Barclays.

If Barclays were to do this, it would be following in the footsteps of Apple's success with iTunes. iTunes has long available for every Mac or Windows computer and is a great way to organize your music. Only later did Apple create the iTunes store and start selling music and iPods there. But because Apple gave iTunes away for free, not only did it give you something great, it also created a huge fan base that it could sell music and iPods to—and had collected enough data on those fans to be able to make offers that would fulfill their needs.

Of course, working with Barclays would make the software even more effective—just like iTunes. The bank could build in all kinds of extra reasons to motivate you to go to Barclays for all of your financial needs. But the beauty lies in the fact that Barclays would truly be supporting small or start-up companies. This would really help the bank take that one small step of turning its current (empty) payoff into an actual giving mission.

Brainstorm #3

Category	Large-scale events
Possible brand	The Olympic Games
Possible brand mission	Inspire a generation
Marketing activation	Instead of just communicating about inspiring a generation, mobilize all of the sponsors to actually make it happen.

During the 2012 London Olympics, I couldn't stop myself from having a go at making the Olympics an even more Social Brand. Watching the irreverent, hilarious, and occasionally brilliant British-themed opening ceremony by Danny Boyle, I couldn't stop thinking about the London 2012 payoff: *Inspire a Generation*. It was a great theme, but the only part of the ceremony where it came into play was the moment that five-time gold medalist Steve Redgrave handed the Olympic torch to a group of next-generation Olympic hopefuls, who in turn lit the Olympic flame. Why didn't Boyle take this further? The rest of the opening ceremony was filled with music (from the Beatles to Dizzee Rascal), business (from the Industrial Revolution to the invention of the Internet), and literature (from Shakespeare to J.K. Rowling). But where was the connection to future generations? How could the London 2012 Olympics have actually inspired *and* enabled them to succeed?

London 2012 could have sat down with its main sponsors and defined these four key areas of Britain's history—sports, music, business, and literature—and given its all to connect them to Britain's future success. Adidas could have taken sports, Coke music, Visa business, and McDonald's literature. Before the opening ceremony, the four sponsors could have defined specific programs for finding and nurturing young talent in each discipline and selected some of the best. Just as with the Olympic flame, today's most successful sports figures, musicians, businesspeople, and writers could have passed the baton to the next generation, giving young, up-and-coming talent some airtime on the largest stage on earth. The inventor of the World Wide Web could have introduced the next start-up from the Old Street Roundabout; J.K. Rowling could have passed a book to a new writing talent who could read a small passage of his or her latest piece. The sponsors would own these areas; even if the sponsors were not explicitly connected with the disciplines in the ceremony, people would know.

After the Olympics, the program could continue by enlisting the help of the London Organising Committee and the British government, whose single biggest concern (after safety) was the legacy of the Games. Creating genuine platforms to help the next generation flourish would be a win-win-win situation—it would give the sponsors great stories, provide great opportunities for the next generation, and give the government exactly what it wants. Some very simple examples of how the Olympics and its sponsors could have built the legacy afterwards:

- Adidas organizes talent scout days in Olympic Park.
- Coke has Mark Ronson (whom it used for the rather poor "Move to the Beat" campaign) support young new musicians by producing the best three albums.
- Visa supports young entrepreneurs with funding and space, just as Telefónica does with its Wayra Academy.

And McDonald's and literature? It might sound like a strange combo deal, but it could prove to be pretty tasty if well executed. Get a great writer, such as J.K. Rowling, on board to mentor talented young writers and produce a book of amazing stories. Instead of taking the easy route of trying to benefit *Ice Age* and its characters, why not use its own characters—created by young talent that walks into its restaurants regularly? These are just some simple examples that I cooked up on my way to work; I'm sure that the chain could generate much better and more polished campaigns. But my key point is: don't just *say* that you want to "inspire a generation"; commit yourself to it *and make it happen*. That's what a Social Brand is about.

Brainstorm #4

Category	Beverages
Possible brand	Budweiser
Possible brand mission	Help people throw the best parties or get-togethers with friends. Many people love to throw parties but often lack the expertise, creativity, or organizational skills to pull it off.
Marketing activation	Budweiser will create the best online platform ever to help people plan their party; they can pick the theme and date and which friends they want to invite over to have a good time.

OK, one last one:

Budweiser's current positioning is "Great times are waiting…grab some Buds." I checked Budweiser's website to see if this is simply a statement (as with so many other brands) or an *actual commitment* to help you have a great time. Unfortunately, it's the former. All the company had on its site was a Facebook app that does no more than invite your friends to a party: select a date and pick your friends, and they'll get an invitation on Facebook. Oddly enough, Facebook already has the *exact same functionality* with its (very often used) "create an event" tab. The Budweiser app adds nothing except its branding.

If the company took its role seriously and really wanted to help people experience great times, it would take that concept and make it into something big. Budweiser could create an online platform that is *the* destination on the Web for organizing get-togethers with friends. It could help people come up with a great theme, location, invitations, and party soundtracks—or even locate a great DJ in the neighborhood. People could automatically generate a personal party page on the Bud website where guests could see all of the event details and possibly their role in the party (perhaps they have to come dressed as somebody special, make a dish for the family meal, etc.). The possibilities are endless.

The company could create all kinds of product tie-ins, such as delivering Buds to the house or venue for bigger parties or putting a "BYOB(udweiser)" request on the invitations for smaller ones. But it's not just about product integration; Budweiser needs to become the expert on having a great time and be the partner that supports people by providing the tools to make that happen. Budweiser would no longer tell folks that great times are waiting (where? when?); it would actually help them create those great times.

I think this is a good example to end the book with. Why? Because it shows that it's not difficult to shift from communicating brand positioning to actually going out and taking an active role. It also shows how little of what's done in the world of marketing is truly giving. The vast majority of brands still do things the old way: position the brand and then hammer that positioning home. But that approach doesn't work anymore; brands need to create a relationship. And the only way to do that is to define a role and then go out and live it. In Budweiser's case, it should be relatively straightforward to do—yet it would be utterly giving and, in the end, very powerful: "Great times are waiting; go to Budweiser.com and we'll help you make them happen."

CHAPTER ELEVEN

Final thoughts

This is a book on marketing and how to grow your business by creating a great product, giving it a Social Brand mission that emphasizes its value, and using giving forms of marketing to communicate that value. Before you put this book down and set about transforming your brand, I'd like to share two final thoughts about giving.

Intention

The first part of giving is intention or motivation. This comes up a lot when brands loudly talk up their CSR programs; you can't help but wonder if they actually care about the cause or are just doing it to increase sales. This relates to Chapter 5, when we talked about defining your brand mission—you have to care about the brand's mission and what it's trying to give. Every giving marketing campaign that I've been involved in fulfilled me tremendously. The people who sent me thank-you mails because the Bertolli dinner website had brought the family back together, the hopeful young musicians who were putting all of their passion and dedication into making their very first video clip that would air on MTV, and the sheer joy of the BMXers riding on their very own dirt track that Red Bull's shapers and machines had built. Offer true value to the people who are important to you—it will inspire you, and it will inspire your company.

There are two reasons why this is very important. First of all, people will notice whether you really mean it or not. If you don't really mean it, your brand personality won't be authentic and people won't accept it—and it certainly won't help build your brand. The second important aspect of motivation is literally your own motivation; you'll put more effort and dedication into something you truly believe in. As Steve Jobs once put it in typically brutal fashion after Microsoft had (unsuccessfully) launched its iPod me-too, Zune:

> *The older I get, the more I see how much motivation matters. The Zune was crappy because the people at Microsoft don't really love music or art the way we do. We win because we personally love music. We made the iPod for ourselves, and when you are doing something for yourself, or your best friend or family, you are not going to cheese out. If you don't love something, you are not going to go the extra mile, work the extra weekend, and challenge the status quo as much.*

If you look at the top ranks of many of the successful companies that headline most of the cool-brands lists, you can always spot an active mission or role that came before there was even a thought of making money. Take Google: its mission is "to organize the world's information and make it universally accessible and useful." It's pretty obvious that Google takes this seriously. We've all searched for things (a good restaurant, a new pair of shoes, an old friend) countless times—and Google has found them for us. That's pure giving that comes from an active role or mission. The same goes for Wikipedia; its mission is "to empower and engage people around the world to collect and develop educational content under a free license in the public domain, and to disseminate it effectively and globally." Again, there are millions and millions of people who have found a useful piece of information because of this clear, active intention. And all free of charge!

Community

The second part of giving is the impact it has on the community, whether that's inspiring and enabling creativity, providing tools to keep people exercising, or keeping older people connected and involved. When you stop asking "How can we make them buy us more?" and start asking "How can we do more for them?", when the positioning that you go out and communicate *becomes* the role that you go out into the world and fulfill, it will have an impact.

If my assumption is correct, about 90% of what we spend on marketing currently goes toward taking forms of marketing; if we were to move the Brand Bank Account balance closer to 50/50, the impact would be massive. Zenith Media indicated that global spending on advertising was $518 billion in 2013 and will rise to around $573 billion in 2015. Now, this is ad spending, of which TV still gets the lion's share. You could say that every penny of this is a form of taking marketing, because it doesn't take into account all of the forms of giving, such as sponsorship, engagement programs, and events. You could even add money to that amount, because that more than half a trillion dollars is just the cost of *buying* the media; it doesn't take into account the actual production of the ads. (Look at your marketing budget—I bet production accounts for a hefty portion of it.) The total probably tops $600 billion. Now let's assume that you spend half of that on giving marketing; that's about the same as the world's most generous country, the US, gives away on philanthropy each year.

And the cherry on top is what it will do for you. There's nothing more rewarding than creating a product, experience, or event that people truly appreciate. Every giving marketing campaign I've been involved with has given me a great sense of fulfillment. It can inspire you and your company, too.

What more could you ask for? Then again, you're no longer *asking* for anything....

Join our community

Visit our website at http://www.TheSocialBrand.co.uk and follow me on Twitter (@huibvanbockel) to:

- Help define the future of *The Social Brand* by sharing your insights and adding your thoughts, ideas, and examples
- Add examples of Social Brands or great marketing deposits
- Communicate with the author
- Purchase additional copies of *The Social Brand*

Acknowledgements

It's taken me quite a while to bring this book from idea to completion. It's been a tough but enjoyable ride; this kind of a project takes a considerable amount of time when combined with a (rather busy) job and a family; it's basically been my holiday hobby to get it all down in writing.

The marketing experts that I would like to thank are David Meerman Scott, author of the bestseller *The New Rules of Marketing & PR*), for the words that got me started; David Taylor, author of *The Brand Gym*, for the words that kept me going and Paul Kemp-Robertson from Contagious for inspiring me with great examples and generally being a massive help in getting this book out.

Then there is of course my wife, Cindy, who had to put up with me—especially because I wrote *The Social Brand* on "our" time during all of our holidays and (not too) occasional weekends in these past years. We were fortunate enough to spend about five months traveling, so there was enough time to write the book and have a great time as well. She has also read and reread my many rewrites. So thanks, honey! To my lovely kids for their constant and very welcome distraction.

Then there were my many marketing friends. Thanks to Jeroen van Eck of the amazing advertising agency Joe Public (http://joepublicamsterdam.nl/) for reading my very first draft and, together with Lies, convincing me to choose a new title. To the inspiring Mie Leng Wong and the brilliant Atif Sheikh for reading and providing great feedback. Later, Robin was a very positive reader who motivated me to keep writing. To my most critical reader, Janti Soeripto, whose sharp feedback led me to streamline the book by cutting about 10,000 words out of the draft. To Mark van de Grift, who motivated me to add some good old diagrams to make it all a bit easier to follow. And to Tijmen Mulder for brainstorming some of the hypothetical examples in Chapter 10 with me.

Tim van Tongeren, thank you for inspiring me to keep going and build my web platform; you've been one of the major *givers* to this book and its web presence and have always been there for me. To be honest, my Brand Bank Account heavily skews in your favor at the moment. Also for hooking me up with my sharp editor, Bill Nagel, who made my personal ramblings readable; thanks to Bill for his amazing contribution and "always ready to help" attitude (Bill, maybe just leave this bit like it is to show people the impact you had ;-) *[Sorry, Huib: editors gotta edit. —B]*

Thanks also to Maartje for her feedback and to Lara Molins Caplin, who as head of PR for my book helped me spread the word. To Mark Adams for our inspiring meetings and boost to build the book. And thanks to Jop Blom, who has been a massive advocate of "Social" and helped spread the word.

The lovely front cover was created by Dann Smit. Thanks for everything, Dann, you were one of the three key people who made this whole venture possible!

And last, of course, my dad. As I mentioned in my foreword, he inspired me to make marketing my profession; he and his father always inspired me to aim high. Without my dad, of course, I would never have been able to write this book.

Thanks to all of you!

Bibliography

Definitions

The Free Dictionary by Farlex: *Social*. (http://www.the-freedictionary.com/social)

Foreword

Gladwell, Malcolm. *Outliers: The Story of Success*. Penguin, 2009.

Chapter 1: It starts with the right question

Deloitte & Touche. "So many apps—so little to download", December 2011.

Nielsen Company, The. *State of the Media: The Social Media Report 2012*, April 2012 (http://www.nielsen.com/us/en/insights/reports/2012/state-of-the-media-the-social-media-report-2012.html).

Wikipedia (http://en.wikipedia.org/wiki/Consumer).

Chapter 2: The start of a new business era

Curtis, Anthony, Ph.D. *The Brief History of Social Media* (http://www.uncp.edu/home/acurtis/NewMedia/SocialMedia/SocialMediaHistory.html).

Kotler, Philip. *Principles of Marketing.* Prentice Hall, 1980.

Nielsen Company, The. *The global, socially conscious consumer, March 2012* (http://www.nielsen.com/us/en/insights/news/2012/the-global-socially-conscious-consumer.html)

Nielsen Company, The. *Doing well by doing good, June 2014* (http://www.nielsen.com/us/en/insights/reports/2014/doing-well-by-doing-good.html)

Chapter 3: The Brand Bank Account: why brands need to stop taking and start giving

Covey, Stephen R. *The 7 Habits of Highly Effective People.* Free Press, 1989.

Gladwell, Malcolm. *Blink: The Power of Thinking Without Thinking.* Penguin, 2005.

Chapter 4: The product: the first deposit

"Online Extra: Q&A with Google's VP of Marketing." *Bloomberg BusinessWeek,* August 5, 2007.

Chima, Chikodi. "Pie In The Sky? Domino's Flips Switch On Times Square Instant Reviews, Takes Transparency To New Level." *Fast Company,* July 25, 2011.

Hansen, Morten T., Herminia Ibarra, and Urs Peyer. "The 100 Best-Performing CEOs in the World." *Harvard Business Review,* January-February 2013.

Millward Brown. *BrandZ™ Top 100: Most Valuable Global Brands 2013* (http://www.millwardbrown.com/brandz/2013/Documents/2013_BrandZ_Top100_Report.pdf).

Roberts, Hannah. "#McFail! McDonalds' Twitter promotion backfires as users hijack #McDstories hashtag to share fast food horror stories." *The Daily Mail,* January 24, 2012.

Roberts, Jeff John. "McDonald's Social Media Director Explains Twitter Fiasco." *paidContent,* January 24, 2012.

Wasserman, Todd. "Domino's Pizza Runs Unfiltered Customer Comments on Times Square Billboard." *Mashable Business,* July 25, 2011.

Chapter 5: Building the brand: from a "positioned brand" to a Social Brand

Botton, Alain de. *Religion for Atheists: A Non-believer's Guide to the Uses of Religion.* Pantheon, 2012.

Hauser, Susan. "Must Be the Shoes." *People,* May 4, 1992.

Isaacson, Walter. *Steve Jobs.* Simon & Schuster, 2011.

Kemp, Nicola. "Six marketing lessons from Red Bull Stratos." *Marketing,* October 19, 2012.

Markowicz, Chloe. "Case Study / Magazine Luiza." *Contagious Magazine,* Q4 2012.

Maslow, Abraham H. *Motivation and Personality.* Harper, 1954.

Nielsen Company, The. *Global Trust in Advertising Survey,* April 2012 (http://www.nielsen.com/us/en/insights/reports/2013/global-trust-in-advertising-and-brand-messages.html).

Strasser, J.B. and Laurie Becklund. *Swoosh: The Unauthorized Story of Nike and the Men Who Played There.* HarperBusiness, 1993.

Trout, Jack. "'Positioning' is a game people play in today's me-too market place." *Industrial Marketing,* Vol. 54, No. 6, June 1969.

Zajonc, Robert B. "Attitudinal Effects of Mere Exposure." *Journal of Personality and Social Psychology,* 9(2), 1968.1968.

Chapter 6: Maximizing the link between brand mission and product

Ben & Jerry's website (http://www.benjerry.com/activism/occupy-movement/).

Dulux website (http://www.letscolourproject.com)

Chapter 7: Marketing activations: make sure you give more than you take

Adobe Systems, *Click Here: The State of Online Advertising,* October 2012 (http://www.adobe.com/aboutadobe/

pressroom/pdfs/Adobe_State_of_Online_Advertising_ Study.pdf).

"Wimbledon sponsorship is invisible but in demand." Carat Blog (http://www.carat.co.uk/blog/wimbledon-sponsorship-is-invisible-but-in-demand/).

"WestJet Airlines Ltd. performs Christmas marketing miracle with viral video." *Financial Post*, December 11, 2013. (http:// business.financialpost.com/2013/12/11/westjet-airlines-ltd-performs-christmas-marketing-miracle-with-viral-video/)

"The Top 100 NGOs 2013." *The Global Journal*, January-February 2013.

Goodier, Holly. *Briefing Spring 2012: The Participation Choice.* BBC Internet Blog, May 4, 2012.

Jana website (http://www.jana.com)
KLM blog. "KLM's social media strategy—Part 1." (http:// blog.klm.com/klm%E2%80%99s-social-media-strategy-part-1/4670/).

Learmonth, Michael. "*Ad Age's* Top Viral Ad Campaigns of 2012." *Ad Age,* December 12, 2012.

The Nivea Sun Alarm, American Express, Halonix and Movember examples were adapted from Contagious Feed, courtesy of Contagious Communications (http://www. contagiousmagazine.com).

Chapter 8: How to reach many people with giving marketing

Christakis, Nicholas A. and James H. Fowler. *Connected: The Surprising Power of Our Social Networks and How They Shape Our Lives.* Little, Brown and Company, 2009.

Dunbar, Robin. *Grooming, Gossip, and the Evolution of Language.* Harvard University Press, 1998.

McDonald, Simon. "How to harness the power of conversations." InSites Consulting, February 8, 2013 (http://www.insites-consulting.com/publications/how-to-harness-the-power-of-conversations/).
"The Wizarding World of Public Relations." *Platform Magazine,* Spring 2011.

Reichheld, Frederick F. "The One Number You Need to Grow." *Harvard Business Review,* December 2003.

Scott, David Meerman. *The New Rules of Marketing & PR: How to Use Social Media, Blogs, News Releases, Online Video, and Viral Marketing to Reach Buyers Directly.* John Wiley & Sons, 2010.

Taylor, David and David S. Nichols. *The Brand Gym: A Practical Workout to Gain and Retain Brand Leadership,* John Wiley & Sons, 2010.

Vogelaar, Rijn. *The Superpromoter: The Power of Enthusiasm.* Palgrave Macmillan, 2011.

Chapter 9: Inspiring examples of giving marketing

Carr, David. "Two Guys Made a Web Site, and This Is What They Got." *The New York Times*, July 9, 2012 (http://mediadecoder.blogs.nytimes.com/2012/07/09/two-guys-made-a-web-site-and-this-is-what-they-got/).

OgilvyOne, "Project Silverline" (http://digitalshots.ogilvydo.com/project-silverline/) and adapted from Contagious Feed, courtesy of Contagious Communications (http://www.contagiousmagazine.com).

Upworthy website (http://www.upworthy.com).

Chapter 10: Four free marketing deposits

Barclays (http://www.barclays.co.uk/Businessbankaccounts/BusinessAccounts/Startupbusinessaccounts/P1242558530035).

Chapter 11: Final thoughts

Isaacson, Walter. *Steve Jobs*. Simon & Schuster, 2011.

"ZenithOptimedia forecasts 4.1% growth in global adspend in 2013", Zenith Optimedia, December 3, 2012 (http://www.zenithoptimedia.com/zenithoptimedia-forecasts-4-1-growth-in-global-adspend-in-2013/)

Index